7 Lessons for New Pastors

7 Lessons for New Pastors

—— Your First Year in Ministry ——

Second Edition

Matthew D. Kim

FOREWORD BY
Scott M. Gibson

CASCADE *Books* • Eugene, Oregon

7 LESSONS FOR NEW PASTORS, SECOND EDITION
Your First Year in Ministry

Cascade Books
An Imprint of Wipf and Stock Publishers
199 W. 8th Ave., Suite 3
Eugene, OR 97401

www.wipfandstock.com

PAPERBACK ISBN: 978-1-7252-6857-9
HARDCOVER ISBN: 978-1-7252-6858-6
EBOOK ISBN: 978-1-7252-6859-3

Cataloguing-in-Publication data:

Names: Kim, Matthew D., author. | Gibson, Scott M., foreword.

Title: 7 lessons for new pastors, second edition : your first year in ministry / by Matthew D. Kim ; foreword by Scott M. Gibson.

Description: Eugene, OR: Cascade Books, 2021 | Includes bibliographical references.

Identifiers: ISBN 978-1-7252-6857-9 (paperback) | ISBN 978-1-7252-6858-6 (hardcover) | ISBN 978-1-7252-6859-3 (ebook)

Subjects: LCSH: Pastoral theology. | Clergy—Office.

Classification: BV4014 .K57 2021 (print) | BV4014 (ebook)

To Sarah—

My partner in life and in ministry

Contents

List of Tables | viii
Foreword by Scott M. Gibson | ix
Acknowledgments | xi
Introduction | xiii

Lesson 1: Be Certain of Your Calling | 1
Lesson 2: Find the Right Church | 17
Lesson 3: Acclimate to the Pastor's Life | 34
Lesson 4: Create Healthy Habits | 56
Lesson 5: Develop Your Leadership Skills | 73
Lesson 6: Love Your Congregation | 89
Lesson 7: Expect the Unexpected | 103

Conclusion | 113

Lesson 7.1: Cultivate Your Character | 119
Lesson 7.2: Practice Your Pastoral Skills | 126

Bibliography | 133

List of Tables

Sample Weekly Schedule | 40

Foreword

A TENSION EXISTS BETWEEN wanting to know the realities of ministry and not desiring to know. We may not mind being blissfully ignorant—until we get into a tough spot and wish we had been told. But, really, do we want to know? Seminarians tend to think in terms of schedules, the classroom, and grades but not necessarily people. Even some pastors are clueless about the intricacies of the pastorate because they don't understand ministry, people, or themselves.

If only we had taken the right seminary course, signed up for the appropriate workshop, attended a helpful conference, or even read the right book! In the classic movie *A Few Good Men*, Lieutenant Daniel Kaffee (Tom Cruise) examined Colonel Nathan R. Jessep (Jack Nicholson) on the witness stand. The dialogue ping-ponged back and forth. "You want answers?" mocked Col. Jessep. "I think I'm entitled to them," shot Lt. Kaffee. "You want answers?" Jessep drilled again, and Kaffee shouted, "I want the truth!" "You can't handle the truth," barreled Jessep.

Do you want answers? Can you handle the truth? I mean the beautifully messy truth of pastoral ministry. Matthew D. Kim tells the truth. He is up front about his first year of pastoral ministry, the lessons he learned from it, and the lessons he continues to learn. These seven lessons are foundational for any new pastor or even the most seasoned veteran: Be certain of your calling, find the right church, acclimate to the pastor's life, create healthy habits, develop your leadership skills, love your congregation, and expect the unexpected.

Matthew Kim's insights will help readers get a head start on the lessons of ministry. Try to read this book not as an academic textbook, as if there'll be a quiz on its contents. Instead, read it as a practical resource, and I can guarantee you that every topic touched on in this helpful book will be field-tested in your life and ministry. Matthew Kim learned big lessons during his first year of ministry that he put into this little volume. These lessons will help you to handle the truth of what it means to be a pastor.

You don't need to resent that you didn't learn in seminary what this book has to share. Nor do you have to search for that ever-elusive workshop or conference. You have the right book in your hands. Matthew Kim has done it. My sentiment is that I wish I could've read this book when I entered the pastorate. And I also wish I had written it. But with fresh eyes and insight Matthew Kim provides a rich resource for any new or experienced pastor.

If I may have liberty with Jesus' words that "the truth will set you free," my hope is that this truth about the beautiful messiness of ministry will not discourage you but encourage you, even embolden you to serve the Lord with wisdom and understanding. Matthew Kim provides the answers and helps readers to handle the truth with grace.

Scott M. Gibson

Professor of Preaching
Holder of the David E. Garland Chair of Preaching
Director of the PhD Program in Preaching
George W. Truett Theological Seminary, Baylor University

Acknowledgments

To the wonderful team at Cascade Books, including Rodney Clapp, Michael Thomson, Matt Wimer, and others, thank you so much for the honor of publishing this second edition and for pooling your collective insights to make the book stronger.

Words cannot convey my gratitude to my mentor, friend, and colleague, Scott M. Gibson, for carefully crafting the Foreword to this book. Thank you, Scott, for your continued encouragement, friendship, and guidance over these many years.

Many other friends and family members have taught me lessons over the years. I am not able to mention them all by name, but here are some individuals who have made a lasting impact on me: Kay Friedrich, Kenneth Hwang, Dennis Kim, Ki Wang and Taek Hee Kim, Timothy Kim, Philip Niles, Chung Hyun and Jung Sook Oh, Soong-Chan Rah, and William Storrar.

I also want to thank Nijay K. Gupta, who offered his time and wisdom about the journey of writing his second edition of *Prepare, Succeed, Advance: A Guidebook for Getting a PhD in Biblical Studies and Beyond* (Cascade, 2019).

Thanks to my wife, Sarah, for her incomparable love and commitment to me and our family. Writing the first edition of *7 Lessons for New Pastors* was her idea, and I must give credit where it's due. Sarah, it's my honor and privilege to dedicate this second edition to you, as well. I love you and thank God for you.

To my dear sons, Ryan, Evan, and Aidan, thanks for reminding me every day of what's really important. I love you more than you will ever know.

Finally, I give praise and thanks to our great Triune God, Father, Son, and Holy Spirit, who called me to ministry. May this book bring glory to you and may it benefit churches around the world as you seek excellence and faithfulness in every pastor.

Introduction

IN THE FIRST EDITION of *7 Lessons for New Pastors*, I wrote from the raw and admittedly tenuous perspective of a newly minted senior pastor. Imagine with me that an author daring to write a bicycle instruction manual had only assembled a few bikes. In many ways, that's how I felt as I was writing the first edition, having had by that time just two or three years of actual full-time senior pastor experience. As the saying goes, "We don't know what we don't know."

As I write this second edition, there are, of course, aspects of the instruction manual that I haven't completely mastered. Like you, I'm a work in progress seeking to move toward Christlikeness. I'm seeking to grow each day as a disciple of Jesus. And yet, I can confidently say that today I have more to share with prospective pastors—lessons learned from the failures and successes of nearly a decade of pastoral ministry experience and another decade of training pastors, preachers, and Christian leaders in a theological seminary context.

The book in your hands is similar to the first edition, but I've gone through it with a fine-tooth comb. Ministry has changed dramatically since I began writing the first edition. As I write this second edition during the Spring of 2020, the COVID-19 pandemic is in full force, changing how we do ministry for the foreseeable future and perhaps altering ministry visions and strategies until Christ returns. To reflect and engage our increasingly diverse world, I'll be sharing the wisdom of pastors, ministry leaders, and authors who come from various denominations, ethnic and cultural backgrounds, and even genders.

Additionally in this second edition, I share observations throughout from the perspective of a seminary professor who trains eager and anxious seminarians who ponder what their lives will be like in the pastorate. Finally, I provide two short bonus lessons not included in the previous edition. My hope is that all of these lessons will embolden you toward joyful ministry service for the long haul. Before we dive into these seven lessons that I learned in my first year of ministry as a senior pastor, I'd like to start by describing seven misconceptions about pastoral ministry. Many of these misconceptions become stumbling blocks for new pastors as their ministries unfold.

Misconceptions in Ministry

Misconception 1: Ministers Have It Easy

Pastors are often the target of jokes in society and in the church. We are frequently portrayed as having it easy. Michael Milton shares: "I once had a young deacon, naïve about the ministry and sadly ignorant about the Word of God, tell me, 'I see you give a speech a couple of times per week and then get all this vacation time. This sounds like a pretty good gig for me! Where do I sign up?'"[1] The general inference is either that pastors don't work very hard or that people only see us working for a handful of hours on Sunday. But I assure you, if done in the appropriate way, pastoral ministry is far from a cozy existence.

Similarly, pastoral ministry is not for the fainthearted. While it produces joy on various levels, the ministry can be a pride-swallowing and thankless calling (more on the topic of calling in lesson 1). It requires immense humility and self-sacrifice. At times, the service of our Lord Jesus Christ warrants sleepless nights, sweat, and tears. Like a twenty-four-hour hotline, our cell phones are always turned on for the unexpected late night call. We witness every day the ugly sores of human depravity mired in ourselves and in others. Pastors bear the secret burdens of broken parishioners. We attempt to balance the impossible: life at home and life at church. In short, people who believe ministry is an easy road do not understand the depths of pastoral work. If we feel that we can coast through the pastorate until our retirement with any real impact or effectiveness, we are greatly mistaken.

1. Milton, "Portrait of a Minister."

If you're considering pastoral ministry or training for a seminary degree with aspirations of the pastorate, please be advised that your life will never be the same again. Yes, the life of pastoral ministry has its benefits. There is some flexibility with time that others don't have. But you will simultaneously enter a world of adversity. We do not enter pastoral ministry for the salary or for the prestige. In fact, Jesus cautioned us in Luke 9:23: "Whoever wants to be my disciple must deny themselves and take up their cross daily and follow me." Don't let this scare you off, but don't be cavalier about it either. Ministry is far from easy. It was never meant to be, and it never will be.

Misconception 2: Ministry Is a Means to an End

The life of a seminary professor is often glorified by seminarians. Like public school teachers, seminary educators appear to have a comfortable life. They teach the same courses each semester, brush up on and rehearse the same lecture notes from years past, and get summers off for recreation, so it seems. Members of a faculty will sit in on departmental and faculty meetings every so often, but relatively speaking, their time is their own. Graduate students preparing for doctoral programs admire, if not worship, the ground on which they walk. And sometimes for the worst, seminary professors can emit the aura that life in the ivory tower is grander or even more meaningful than life as a minister of the gospel. When I was in seminary, there were even some professors who indirectly conveyed that "if you do a good job in church ministry for a few years, then God might even grant you a teaching post in the future." The implication was that serving God in academia held more gravitas than serving God's people in the local church.

As such, many of my seminary classmates began to view pastoral ministry as a means to the academic guild and not as an end in itself. We know from our classroom experience that training future pastors requires pastoral experience. The most effective seminary professors were those who spent time "in the trenches" of ministry either serving in the church or on the mission field. Yet, the danger is when seminarians "put in their time" in the pastorate for the sake of experience, but they actually want to teach in a Bible college or seminary. In other words, they don't put their heart into it. This ephemeral attitude toward church ministry stymies your overall ministry effectiveness and also dampens the spirit of the congregation you serve. The people will know.

I confess that similar thoughts crossed my mind sometimes during seminary. I was encouraged by my mentor, Scott M. Gibson, to continue studying for a PhD in homiletics. By God's grace, I spent the next few years after the MDiv working toward a doctorate at the University of Edinburgh in Scotland. I think Scott was grooming me to one day train the next generation of pastoral leaders. In God's providence, I eventually went on to do exactly that. But, this was not my original intention. When I accepted the call to serve my church as a senior pastor, I went to the church indefinitely. There was no timetable and no personal agenda. I wasn't doing ministry to fulfill a quota or go through a hoop to eventually teach. In fact, I had wanted to remain there for fifteen to twenty years or as long as God permitted. However, it became clear after six years of serving as a senior pastor of that congregation that God was setting me on a new trajectory of seminary teaching.

The time that I served in the pastorate was invaluable—both shaping and forming my character and my soul. There was much joy and laughter as well as many tears shed during those years in the pastorate. The members of the congregation became like a family to me. The appreciation that I have for the pastorate has not waned or wavered. I believe wholeheartedly in the local church despite a shift toward training future ministry leaders. Whenever possible, I tell my students to go be the best pastors and preachers they can be. I seldom recommend to students that they pursue the world of academics. My encouragement to seminarians and new pastors is not to view pastoral ministry as a means to another end. Ministry is always the end!

Misconception 3: Pastors Grow the Church

During my childhood, my parents, who were immigrants to this country, worked two jobs to put food on the table. Consequently, my maternal grandmother raised my two younger brothers and me. Grandma became a devout Christian in the second half of her life after converting from Buddhism. I've never known a person who loved to read the Bible more than her. She read through the entire Scripture two to four times per year.

Every day, she taught us biblical principles. One afternoon, I was finished with lunch and was about to race out the front door to play with friends. Grandma looked at my unfinished plate and commented, "Matt, I see that you left some rice. You better eat the rest." I jolted back, "But Grandma, there's hardly anything left on my plate. What's the big deal?"

And she asked a question I won't forget: "Can you make rice grow?" I said, "No, I can't." She smiled and said, "Then you better eat it with joy, because only God can make things grow."

Grandma's loving advice on finishing our plates reflects a fundamental truth about pastoral ministry. As much as pastors would like to believe that we are skillfully trained in the Scriptures and possess mesmerizing personalities to multiply the church, the simple fact is that we can't. Only God can cause a church to grow. And it only happens in his time, and only if he chooses.

Every Sunday, I prayed that God would fill the pews so that his people received encouraging words to live another week. When I began serving the church, we had thirty-five adults and about twenty children. The pews were relatively empty. Eventually, we grew to eighty to ninety consistent adult attenders. During the first year, I took church attendance personally. We know pastors struggle with insecurity: "Maybe there's something wrong with me. Maybe they don't like my preaching. Maybe I'm not relatable enough." Ministry can become self-focused and all about me.

What I learned the hard way is that I couldn't cultivate a church spiritually or numerically. I was powerless to build God's church. It's not about me. It's about God. Though tough to swallow, this truth became refreshing tonic for my depleted soul. God was in full control of this congregation. He would not allow his church to fail. And it grew not by my might, but by his spirit, only if he willed. The words of Jesus in Matthew 16:18 remind us of our helplessness: "And I tell you that you are Peter, and on this rock I will build my church, and the gates of Hades will not overcome it." While we give ministry our best effort, only he can make the church grow.

Misconception 4: God Needs Us to Be Pastors

I once heard prudent advice from a trusted friend: "Don't believe your own press." Another friend used to say to me, "Don't take yourself so seriously." They're both absolutely correct. When we start believing what others say about us, in particular, people's kudos, the sin of pride creeps in. Maybe those friends saw flawed characteristics in me that I couldn't see for myself. The same is true for taking ourselves too seriously. We start to believe that God needs us to serve him in pastoral ministry. We become puffed up with self-glory. We become narcissists.[2] Simultaneously, we mustn't take

2. DeGroat, *When Narcissism Comes to Church.*

too seriously the biting words of our critics. Many detractors speak out of spite or envy, but they don't have our best interests at heart. Their words are toxic, and they are meant to cripple us from doing the Lord's work.

Although it may come as a blow to our egos, God does not in any way, shape, or form require us to fulfill his purposes in this world. God never did. God never will. The church that we lead doesn't need our services for it to thrive. It can carry on just fine without us at the helm or even serving behind the scenes. That is comforting news. Yet in his grace, God selects certain individuals as ministers of the gospel. We're fortunate if he calls us.

The God of the Bible also doesn't require us to preach his word or to sing his praises. In the book of Numbers, Balaam's poor donkey endured an awful beating because of Balaam's pride and spiritual blindness. In that journey, God opened the mouth of a donkey to speak words of truth into Balaam's life and to divert him from a treacherous path. Yet sometimes our vanity gets in God's way, and God eagerly jogs our memories about who we are without him. What this Old Testament narrative conveys is our human futility. God works fine without my humble attempts at pastoral service.

We need God in all areas of our lives. We need God not because we hold the title of pastor but because life cannot be lived apart from God. We crave God's wisdom, God's strength, and God's power in every aspect of our lives. For Jesus said in John 15:5, "I am the vine; you are the branches. If you remain in me and I in you, you will bear much fruit; apart from me you can do nothing."

If we try to lead God's flock without placing him at the center, we will sputter out quickly. John Galloway, Jr. confirms: "*Rather we are acknowledging that God is God and we are not*. God is the creator of the entire cosmos, and God will be God when the last human breath is exhaled on the planet. Our efforts are feeble attempts to do our best in our time. The end result of our labors, however, is beyond our control."[3] Try doing ministry in your own strength for just one Sunday, and you'll know exactly what Galloway means.

Misconception 5: Ministry Is a Sprint and Includes a Silver Bullet

When I was in middle school, I joined both the cross-country and track teams. As a member of the cross-country team, one of the requirements

3. Galloway, Jr., *Ministry Loves Company*, 115.

was to run four miles every weekday whether rain or shine. The goal was obviously to build endurance. Some of my fellow runners had been at this for some time. They could run four miles as easily as the rest of us can eat a pint of our favorite ice cream.

I labored those initial times my feet hit the pavement. I was in horrible shape. On occasion, I would dash to the front just to know what it felt like to be at the head of the pack. But I would quickly trail off, lagging behind by a hundred feet or more. What I realized was that I needed to run at my tempo. If I tried to sprint even a few blocks, I got fatigued. I didn't have to concern myself with how fast others were going. What mattered was that I finished the run and gave it my best effort. As I slowly built up stamina and speed, I was able to finish fifth in our district's final heat. Sprinting full blast was never the answer. Keeping my head up and running diligently to the finish line was the key.

As we begin pastoral ministry, there is an irresistible temptation to sprint. I was fortunate enough to run the one-hundred-yard dash on our track team. Sprinters give it their all for about twelve seconds. The race is all or nothing. Unlike running a 5K or a half marathon, there is no room for reflection. Just run! The same holds true for sprinting in the pastorate. New pastors want to see instant transformation and receive instant gratification. We want to implement the twenty visions that we envisage for Church X all in the first year. New ministers overzealously work seventy or eighty hours per week to the abandonment of their families and personal health. We quickly modify or jettison the church's traditions or ministry programs, because we think we know what's best for this church. And sadly, we will either exit the race due to a muscle cramp, or worse, be banned from running altogether.

If we see ministry not as a sprint but as a marathon, we will endure the difficult seasons of pastoral life. I tried my best to pace myself. But that doesn't mean I didn't fall down. I still have the scars to prove it. There were palpable moments of fatigue and burnout. Yet I learned to pick my battles. I chose to speak my mind when the occasion called for it, but I also knew when it was time to release my grip. Ministry far exceeded my limited understanding of where this church should go. Pushing a personal agenda got me nowhere.

Ministry is predicated on God using us in the slow, persistent, taxing, daily grind of ministry service. Another metaphor is that ministry does not include an automatic silver bullet. As Daniel Im contends, "The myth of the silver bullet is alive and well—and it's not because of old reruns of *The Lone Ranger*, or teenage novels about werewolves. It's alive and well because we want the quick fix. We have been conditioned for the instant. It's our hidden addiction."[4] Advancement in technology has reinforced this instantaneous growth mentality. If I plug in successful ministry program X, borrowed from the latest leadership conference, it should immediately result in ministry productivity Y. We get impatient when the information we seek doesn't pop up in five seconds in our search engines. Ministry is not a sprint. It's a marathon of marathons. It takes years, decades, and even lifetimes. I'm simply called to run with my parishioners toward the finish line. It's all about Jesus Christ and his bride, the church. We are simply called to finish the race.

Misconception 6: Pastors Are Perfect, but Members Are Not

Every pastor struggles with personal integrity and holiness issues. We strive for God's standards to be our own, but we recognize our limitations. We are sinners, too. When's the last time you read through the list of qualifications for an elder from 1 Timothy 3 or Titus 2? However, we are prone to show ourselves grace quickly and freely. We pat our backs for even mentioning Leviticus 19:2 on our to-be list. Our internal monologue tells us that our imperfection is tolerable. Pastors are only human, we say. And we give ourselves the grace to see another day.

Yet when it comes to the members of our church, their imperfections stick out like unsightly blemishes on a forehead. Don't they understand the heart of God? God holds Christians to higher standards. Our mantra becomes, "Why don't you get it? Why can't you change?" Our frustration with others' sins overwhelms us to the point that we bounce from church to church hoping that somewhere people will live out what we teach them.

Finger pointing is part and parcel of being human. "I'm not the problem; they are," we say. Yet in his Sermon on the Mount, Jesus asked the crowd the following in Matthew 7:3–5: "Why do you look at the speck of sawdust in your brother's eye and pay no attention to the plank in your own eye? How can you say to your brother, 'Let me take the speck out of your eye,' when all the time there is a plank in your own eye? You hypocrite, first

---

4. Im, *No Silver Bullets*, 4.

take the plank out of your own eye, and then you will see clearly to remove the speck from your brother's eye."

We're also reminded of the Apostle Paul's humble confessions in 1 Timothy 1:15–16 to his young protégé Timothy about acknowledging sin: "Here is a trustworthy saying that deserves full acceptance: Christ Jesus came into the world to save sinners—of whom I am the worst. But for that very reason I was shown mercy so that in me, the worst of sinners, Christ Jesus might display his immense patience as an example for those who would believe in him and receive eternal life."

God has reminded me of my imperfections through my astute wife. One day, as a pastor, when I was venting my frustrations about our church members' inability to change, she offered sobering words of wisdom: "How difficult is it for you to change in your areas of weakness? In the same way, try to show them the same level of grace and patience you award yourself." She continued, "You wish God gave you a wife that just told you what you want to hear, right?" And I smugly replied with a grin, "Yes!" The real answer is a "No." Change takes time in the life of a church just as it does in my own. What our parishioners require from us is not a critical eye but rather love and patience. Changing them is God's responsibility, not ours.

Misconception 7: Ministry Isn't That Joyful

I once met a younger pastor whose role was to shepherd college students and young adults in his congregation. His attitude toward ministry was commendable and worth sharing. In the course of our conversation he said something that I'll never forget: "I have so much fun being a pastor. I can't believe that they pay me to do this!" With all its challenges and irritations, pastoral ministry should elicit joy.

If we will serve God faithfully and love our people without reservation, our ministry will be a source of elation. At times, ministry brings laughter as we celebrate our congregants' accomplishments and blessings. We cheer for their success from the sidelines. And yet we also fight alongside them when they experience valleys. They may invite us to share intimate hardships that they will communicate with no one else. In short, they allow us to have a piece of their souls. There is no greater joy on this side of heaven than being a minister of the gospel of our Lord Jesus Christ. Will you take a moment now to thank God for the ministry that he has entrusted to you?

May we thank God for this tremendous opportunity and privilege of serving him in this unique way.

Conclusion

If you're holding this book, you've probably sensed God's call on your life to join him on a wonderful journey called pastoral ministry. Perhaps you're a seminarian in the process of training for a life of ministerial service or a pastoral candidate searching for your first position out of seminary. You're thrilled as you dream about how God will use your gifts and talents in a local church. One day a church member will call you Pastor, and it might come as a shock to you. The reality will set in that you have been entrusted with the lives of real congregants. You may wonder what this life will look like on a daily basis. Anxiety may creep in as you consider the challenges that await you as a new pastor traveling unchartered waters.

This book chronicles my early experiences when I served as a senior pastor. It documents my failures and successes as I tried to navigate the contours of the first year of pastoral ministry. My experiences are my own and will not mirror the complexities of your situation. Each church is unique. However, I hope to guide you as a future minister in preparing mentally, emotionally, physically, and spiritually for that very important first year of the pastorate and beyond.

In order to minister effectively, we should understand what we're getting ourselves into. And that's exactly where we're headed. These seven lessons cover topics on the beginnings of ministry that will open our eyes to life in the pastorate: Be certain about your calling, find the right church, acclimate to the pastor's life, create healthy habits, develop your leadership skills, love your congregation, and expect the unexpected. As mentioned, this second edition also includes two short bonus lessons: cultivate your character and practice your pastoral skills. Although it is not meant to be comprehensive in nature, this work will offer you encouragement and practical tools as you get started. Let's begin by confirming our call to the ministry.

1

Be Certain of Your Calling

A Mother's Dedication

WHEN I WAS TEN years old, my mother shared with me the story of my near-death experience. This tragic event occurred on the day of my birth. During the course of delivery, the obstetrician operated with unhygienic forceps to draw me out of my mother's womb. The forceps severed my scalp on every side. Those cuts soon morphed into a vicious infection. After a few months, even specialists confirmed that there would be no chance of survival. Thus, in an act of great desperation, my mother pleaded with God to intervene. She dedicated my future to full-time pastoral ministry. Her decision forever altered my plot in life. At least, it has often seemed that way.

As a child, my Sunday school teachers sought to bring biblical characters to life. The people who were similarly dedicated to the Lord's service by their parents were especially captivating. For instance, I remember learning about Hannah, who set apart Samuel for the Lord's work. In 1 Samuel 1:27–28, Hannah said, "I prayed for this child, and the LORD has granted me what I asked of him. So now I give him to the LORD. For his whole life he will be given over to the LORD."

Obviously, major differences exist between my humble beginnings and Samuel's. First, my mother dedicated her firstborn son whom she almost lost after childbirth, whereas Hannah committed her child out of her inability to conceive. Second, Samuel is one of the greatest prophets of the Old Testament, and my origins pale in comparison to his prominent life's work.

Yet rather than appreciating my mother's prayer and thanking God for sparing my life, I spent a significant portion of my early years questioning my mother's actions. Why did I not have a say in all this? Growing up, I had grand visions of becoming a Supreme Court Justice or a professional baseball player. However, those aspirations were shattered in that act of dedication—even if they were merely childhood dreams. I spent much of my earlier years rebelling against this ministerial path prescribed for me.

It would be an entire decade before a pivotal event brought forth great appreciation for what God had done through my mother's valiant prayer, and it sent me to my knees in humble submission to God's calling for my life. (I will recount this story later.) If you are considering ministry as your vocation, this lesson speaks to the magnitude of being absolutely certain of your calling.

Confusion about One's Calling

For most seminary applications, I would assume that potential seminarians are asked to describe their calling experience. What do people write down as their testimony? Was it a supernatural burning bush experience akin to Moses's story? Perhaps it was a logical conversation with a trusted friend that led someone to realize their gift for ministry. Maybe it was a fiery sensation in one's heart to make disciples for Jesus Christ. Over the years I have witnessed an ever-growing population of seminarians who enter parish ministry without a clear conviction of their call. The number of students who have questions about the call or question their calling is astounding. "How did you know that you were called?" they ask. It may be the number one issue that comes up during office hours or in casual conversations.

What is clear is that much confusion abounds in today's seminaries about this issue of calling. For many, it's a difficult concept to pin down. E. Glenn Wagner shares this story:

> A good friend of mine who used to teach at a well-known evangelical seminary once asked several of his classes, "Can you identify a sense of call to ministry?" Most of his students met the question with blank stares. Only about 30 percent in his most "enlightened" class could answer this question in the affirmative, while a scant 4 percent in his most uninformed class could say "yes."[1]

---

1. Wagner, *Escape from Church, Inc.*, 155.

Despite their uncertainty, people still feel set apart for the pastorate, although the numbers are shrinking. Inevitably, there will be some traveling down this path toward full-time ministry who learn the hard way that they were not truly called by God in this way. We've all known friends in seminary who've called it quits. More than the actual tediousness of completing academic exercises, it was often a lack of clear conviction about the call. Allan Hugh Cole, Jr. observes,

> Sometimes students will even begin to question their vocation, speculating if coming to seminary was right for them after all, asking if they are "cut out" for parish ministry, wondering if they are "thick skinned" enough to lead others in faith, and growing uneasy about whether they "know enough" to serve as a pastor amid all the demands they have found out the ministerial life tends to bring.[2]

During my first year in seminary, I lived on a dormitory floor with thirty male seminarians. I will spare you the details of the lack of cleanliness and the musty stench that skulked in the common space, bathroom, and showers. As time went on, several of these floor mates began to sense that the pastorate was not for them. Some opted out of seminary to transfer to law school or to pursue a non-seminary graduate degree. Others decided to work in parachurch organizations. A few even abandoned their faith in Jesus Christ altogether. The bottom line is that they were not called by God to enter the pastorate.

The office of pastor is unlike any other profession. Whether we admit it or not, we can negatively impact the people seated in our church's pews. The seriousness of pastoral ministry cannot be understated. For those not truly called by God, it is wise to get out before we potentially destroy a church and perhaps even damage our faith in the process.

What Does It Mean to Be Called?

In the Old Testament, God used the Hebrew verb *qara* to indicate his unique calling on certain persons for his service. For example, in reference to God, William Mounce observes, "And when he calls someone, he expects that person to answer to his call; anything less is disobedience. This

2. Cole, Jr., ed., *From Midterms to Ministry*, xx.

use can be compared to the contemporary notion of a person being called by God to teach and preach his Word."[3]

The New Testament counterpart is the Greek verb *kaleo*, which means "to call, invite, summon."[4] Mounce notes, "When Jesus began his ministry, he 'called' his disciples (Mt. 4:21; Mk. 1:20). This was a call to physically come to Jesus, but the more important element was a spiritual call, which the disciples heeded."[5] According to these biblical examples, one's calling to ministry was an act evoked by God and adhered to by the recipient of that call.

Is an ordained pastor's calling different from the universal calling of Christians to love and serve the body of Christ? In *Resurrecting Excellence*, L. Gregory Jones and Kevin Armstrong state, "[The pastoral ministry] is a vocation that is intrinsically bound up with the shaping of character, a calling to a particular way of life. It is a profession with high standards of competence and performance."[6] Is ministerial calling differentiated strictly by behavioral ethics and moral codes? Are there additional considerations we may have overlooked? Jeff Iorg suggests the following: "God's call is often found at the intersection of our passion and the opportunities he allows. When ministry is your passion, it may be an indication God is calling you to ministry leadership. If you can't imagine a more fulfilling life than one devoted to leading people in ministry, God may be calling you."[7] In *Now That I'm Called*, Kristen Padilla observes, "We should start by comparing what we think God is calling us to do against the truth God has revealed in Scripture. We should listen to what other believers are telling us, and we should think about our sense of calling in consideration of our spiritual gifts."[8]

An enduring definition of calling comes from Erwin Lutzer, who suggests three dimensions for prayerful consideration. He writes, "God's call is an inner conviction given by the Holy Spirit and confirmed by the Word of God and the body of Christ."[9] Lutzer explains what he means: "First, it is an inner conviction. Feelings and hunches come and go. . . . Second, the Word of God must confirm our call. We have to ask whether a person has

---

3. Mounce, ed., *Mounce's Complete Expository Dictionary*, 92.

4. Mounce, ed., *Mounce's Complete Expository Dictionary*, 93.

5. Mounce, ed., *Mounce's Complete Expository Dictionary*, 93.

6. Jones and Armstrong, *Resurrecting Excellence*, 109.

7. Iorg, *Is God Calling Me?*, 76.

8. Padilla, *Now That I'm Called*, 15. See also Ward, *I Am a Leader*.

9. Lutzer, *Pastor to Pastor*, 11.

the qualifications listed in 1 Timothy 3. . . . Third, the body of Christ helps us understand where we fit within the local church framework."[10]

Lutzer's definition of calling is both tangible and enriching. It's an effective starting point to gauge some essentials of one's call to the ministry. He recognizes that God's calling is an internal conviction, something testable with Scripture and confirmed by members of the church. Each of these components is critical to our understanding of our pastoral calling. My colleague Jim Singleton uses the helpful image of a three-legged stool to illustrate these three essential elements of one's calling. Each leg of the stool is vital for it to support the person sitting on it.

First, we must undergo conviction in our hearts to serve God in this capacity. It's too arduous a road not to be absolutely certain. Though multifaceted, this inner conviction is a passion to preach the gospel as well as a burden to save lost souls. It's what drives discipleship both personally and corporately. Only our God-given zeal and assurance will allow us to persevere especially during turbulent times in our ministries. One person explained it clearly when he shared with me, "If you can see yourself doing anything else, then go do that instead. Don't go into ministry."

Second, as ministers of the gospel, we should measure up to God's qualifications for elders. In particular, using the language of overseers, Paul writes in 1 Timothy 3:2–7:

> Now the overseer is to be above reproach, faithful to his wife, temperate, self-controlled, respectable, hospitable, able to teach, not given to drunkenness, not violent but gentle, not quarrelsome, not a lover of money. He must manage his own family well and see that his children obey him, and he must do so in a manner worthy of full respect. (If anyone does not know how to manage his own family, how can he take care of God's church?) He must not be a recent convert, or he may become conceited and fall under the same judgment as the devil. He must also have a good reputation with outsiders, so that he will not fall into disgrace and into the devil's trap.

Paul offers tangible guidelines for us to mull over, and we should evaluate ourselves based on these biblical principles. While nobody is perfect, pastors should strive to embody the composite of these characteristics.

Lastly, our pastoral calling involves affirmation from the flock. If we don't receive that confirmation from a local congregation, we cannot exercise

---

10. Lutzer, *Pastor to Pastor*, 11–13.

legitimate leadership in a church. Lisa Wilson Davison felt called to ecclesial ministry. However, over time, Davison found that God did not call her to the pastorate, but rather to fulfill her calling in a teaching position at a seminary.[11] Davison understood that one can only be a pastor if a church calls on that person to shepherd them. Ultimately, as part of the discernment process, ask trusted friends and mentors what path you should follow. As you pray, listen to their wise counsel and wait for God's direction.

When one is truly called by God, she may try to flee from it. But in the end, all who are truly called will inevitably serve him. God will see to it. And the evidence of genuine calling is that we will want to do nothing else with our lives. Michael Todd Wilson and Brad Hoffman maintain that "a man or woman truly called of God into the ministry will never be at peace pursuing anything other than what God has called them to do."[12] The good news is that God will be with us at all times.

Reasons to Avoid Pastoral Ministry

Many young, impressionable souls are encouraged to enter ministry without personally discerning their calling. While some prosper in ministry, others leave the pastorate or become bitter toward the Christian faith. There are many reasons to avoid pastoral ministry unless you're called by the Lord. If you are pursuing ministry for any of the following reasons, take a step back and reflect deeply on your motives.

Encouragement or Pressure from Others

A common rationale for pursuing ministry is the encouragement or even pressure received from relatives, friends, or pastors. In his book *Pastor to Pastor*, Erwin Lutzer writes,

> I can remember many young men in Bible college and seminary discussing whether they were "called." Many of them hoped they were called but they weren't sure. . . . One man, burned out at age forty, concluded that he had never been called to the ministry; he entered the ministry only to satisfy his mother. As a youngster he showed great promise in public speaking and church ministry, so

---

11. Davison, *Preaching the Women of the Bible*, 3.
12. Wilson and Hoffman, *Preventing Ministry Failure*, 71.

she encouraged him to become a pastor. Now he concludes that was a mistake.[13]

It's flattering to hear that we exhibit qualities of a good minister. Pastors, for the most part, can have the reputation of being eloquent, encouraging, and motivational, among other complimentary traits. Yet the simple opinion of others isn't a valid incentive to enter pastoral service even if this nudge of confidence comes from your mom or dad.

Another similar reason not to enter the pastorate is merely basing the decision on what we or others perceive to be pastoral gifts. Whether the gifting is related to teaching, preaching, hospitality, interpersonal skills, oral or written communication, musical talent, listening skills, knack for counseling, or any other "ministry" gift, possessing these gifts alone does not validate one's calling to the pastorate. Even if we've been blessed by God with myriad pastoral skills, we should test ourselves based on Lutzer's guidelines to determine the validity of our calling.

It's a Respectable, Professional Job

Another popular justification for entering pastoral ministry is that it's considered venerable work. During my years in seminary, I went home for school breaks to help my parents at their business. Customers would often ask me about my career goals. When I told them I was training to become a pastor, their response was often, "Isn't that nice? Good for you." In other words, people tend to view full-time church work as a meager profession that is somewhat honorable. E. Glenn Wagner describes an exchange between his seminary faculty colleague and a student: "When he asked one student, 'Why are you attending seminary?' the young man replied, 'So I can enter into a respectable, calm, professional ministry to provide for my family.'"[14]

Ministers have various perspectives when it comes to their under-standing of the pastorate as a vocation. For one cluster, there is a growing trend toward self-trained or church-trained clergy who never set foot in a seminary. They are suspicious because they view seminaries as antiquated institutions that don't understand culture and ministry in the real world. They can do just fine in ministry sans a seminary education—perhaps even

13. Lutzer, *Pastor to Pastor*, 10.
14. Wagner, *Escape from Church, Inc.*, 155.

better. There are other pastors who see church ministry as a professional job and therefore pursue seminary degrees much like corporate executives get an MBA or a DBA as a way to bolster their titles and their pay grade. A third category of pastors see their role as a "doctor of souls"[15] who do their best to live out God's instructions for pastoral leaders to care for the congregation as in passages like Hebrews 13:17, where it says: "Obey your leaders and submit to them, for they are keeping watch over your souls, as those who will have to give an account" (ESV).

The first group observes that many of America's largest churches are led by ministers with minimal to zero theological training. Those with barely a bachelor's degree can be employed as a niche pastor or even a senior pastor in a large church and earn a very handsome living. For example, our congregation brought on board a full-time associate/worship pastor. This individual would be responsible for training the praise team, directing the singing portion of the worship service, assisting with preaching/teaching duties, and providing pastoral care. Although the position called for a seminary degree, we received dozens of inquiries from those without any theological background and little training pertinent to ministerial work. One applicant had a culinary arts degree and no other educational or theological credentials, and yet he had served previously as a worship pastor.

Second, those pastors who pursue theological training as stepping stones for ministerial gain need to be circumspect about their motives. I am in full support of receiving additional theological education. It is of great benefit to the congregations we serve. At the same time, however, one must question his or her motives when pursuing theological degrees for pastoral titles rather than increased pastoral service. We have all probably known some pastors who ask, expect, or even demand to be called "doctor" after completing their Doctor of Ministry (DMin) degree. Commensurately, they may want a salary increase or additional pastoral perks, because they have earned the professional title of "doctor." When such self-serving demands surface, sometimes even without our own cognizance, pastors should take time to question what's going on in their hearts.

Third, we've heard the comparisons made between ministers and physicians. Both professions attempt to heal those entrusted to their care. The former is concerned with spiritual healing, while the other is concerned with physical healing. Most of us wouldn't consult a physician who didn't complete medical school. For some reason, however, the church of God is

15. Senkbeil, *The Care of Souls*, 71.

more than willing to enlist pastors simply because they are good communicators and business savvy, all the while failing to demonstrate adequate biblical, theological preparation or even godly, Christian character (see Lesson 7.1). This is a grave travesty in the life and history of the American church. I agree with John Buchanan, who says, "I personally wish theological education would be more demanding, seminaries more selective. I personally wish it were more, not less, difficult to complete the academic preparation the church has always said is the prerequisite for ordination."[16]

At the same time, may we not enter the pastorate simply because it's a respectable vocation that can lead to career advancement. I would assume that most people reading this book either are enrolled in seminary or have concluded their ministry studies. I highly commend you for taking the time, financial resources, and sacrifice to become properly equipped to teach and preach God's word. However, I remind you that pastoral work is unlike the professional world of corporate ladder climbing.

Ministry is not just a respectable vocation. It is our God-given calling. It's a calling that we must treat with utmost respect. To be a pastor is dissimilar from secular or marketplace employment because pastors are inherently servants. As Siang-Yang Tan reminds us, "Yet it is still important to emphasize that a pastor or church leader is primarily a shepherd (or undershepherd) of God's people, or the church. The pastor is a faithful and fruitful *servant* of Jesus Christ and his church, before any leadership models or roles are assumed."[17] Finally, as Derek Prime and Alistair Begg assert, "The ministry of undershepherds and teachers is not simply a job. Rather it is a vocation, the answering of a specific call from God. It is the highest calling in Christian service."[18]

Pursuit of Personal Glory and Fame

Similarly, pastors today are enticed by self-glorification. One does not have to look far to see Christian publishers and media's glamorization of successful pastors. Not only are there several megachurches in every major city, but also television networks and radio shows provide weekly broadcasts of sermons preached by various well-known preachers. The

---

16. Buchanan, foreword to *Ministry Loves Company*, xi.

17. Tan, *Shepherding God's People*, 7.

18. Prime and Begg, *On Being a Pastor*, 17.

crowds seated in the pews are cosmic, and we can often wonder what it feels like to preach to such masses.

Our small congregation once visited a nearby church facility since we needed greater classroom space. We were hoping to rent the building, but it was significantly larger than our needs—spanning 70,000 square feet. The worship sanctuary seated over 1,000 people. With the excitement of little children, my church members wanted me to stand at the pulpit to see what it would look like for their pastor to grace such a large platform. I spent a brief moment at the pulpit and felt an overwhelming sense of pride and curiosity, wondering why I wasn't at the helm of a larger congregation. I arrogantly mused, "I consider myself a good preacher. Why don't I lead a church of this size?" It's extremely attractive to stand in front of such a large assembly and have hundreds and even thousands hearing what you have to say.

Just to be clear, pastoral ministry is not a glamorous position. Most new pastors enter ministry contexts where congregations are few in number and pastors are not in the spotlight. For instance, the Association of Religion Data Archives informs that over 87 percent of churches have less than 250 members.[19] As such, John Galloway, Jr. comments, "Ministry is not meant to be a glitzy, high-roller lifestyle in the fast lane."[20] Eugene Peterson agrees: "Pastoral work is that aspect of Christian ministry which specializes in the ordinary."[21] Further, in *Shepherding the Small Church*, Glenn Daman says, "In an age of specialization, the small church values and utilizes generalists who can do a number of different jobs and responsibilities."[22] Oftentimes, especially for solo pastors, ministry is about the banal: pushing the papers on your desk, answering phone calls, responding to emails, studying the Bible and commentaries for hours on end, visiting the sick, running around to buy supplies for ministry events, and even the manual labor of cleaning the church's toilets.

If we enter ministry for personal glory or fame, we will inevitably be disappointed. There were many Sundays where I was the last person to leave, usually cleaning the church building, picking last-minute scraps off the floor in the fellowship hall and nursery. Christian ministry is about service rendered to God and his people. It's not about our fondness for self-promotion. Make sure you have a sober perspective before you enter

19. See Association of Religious Data Archives at www.thearda.com.
20. Galloway, Jr., *Ministry Loves Company*, 2.
21. Peterson, *Five Smooth Stones for Pastoral Work*, 1.
22. Daman, *Shepherding the Small Church*, 50.

any ministry position. As Jesus said, "So the last will be first, and the first will be last" (Matt 20:16).

Temptation to Quit in the First Years

It's easy to become disillusioned when ministry turns out differently from what we envisioned. As stated in the Introduction, disappointment can be triggered by our misconceptions of what pastoral ministry will entail. Thomas Long writes, "Ministers went to theological school because they had a vision of themselves as change agents, but they often find that real ministry involves being chaplains to narcissists, and they soon grow tired and become discouraged."[23] In similar fashion, David Hansen in *The Art of Pastoring* warns:

> The temptation to quit comes early. . . . We lust after a job in which we could turn stones into bread. Pastors really do have the ability to turn stones into bread. Anyone smart enough to pastor a church successfully could pursue almost any career for better money and fewer hassles. . . . I've never met anyone who had left the ministry but was tempted to go back. Meanwhile, almost every pastor I know is tempted to get out. Every pastor is tempted to break the fast and turn stones into bread.[24]

Only when we are 100 percent committed to and convinced of our calling can we persist in the ministry of the church. As Michael Jinkins states, "If God did not call you to ordained ministry, you really are on your own. And that's not really where you want to be, because you can't do this on your own."[25] There will be moments early on and throughout the pastorate where the demands of the call are overpowering. We feel as if we are barely treading water. For pastors heeding God's call, William Willimon offers these words: "The pastoral ministry is a gift of God to the church. It is not an easy vocation, this calling full of peril. Yet it is also a great gift to have one's life caught up in such a pilgrimage."[26] Don't leave your church and flock prematurely. Stick it out, if you can! The most grueling of circumstances can be trounced with the power of our God

---

23. Long, "Essential Untidiness of Ministry," 9.

24. Hansen, *Art of Pastoring*, 64.

25. Jinkins, *Letters to New Pastors*, 5.

26. Willimon, *Pastor*, 12.

through prayer. Resist the temptation to exit early. Like he did for the Israelites, God fights on your behalf.

So What Kind of Pastor Are You Called to Be?

As you solidify your calling, what type of pastor will you be? That sounds like a peculiar question, but it is crucial for you to think about it and plan ahead. Specifically, will you serve God full-time as a senior pastor, an executive pastor, a campus pastor, an associate pastor, a worship pastor, an outreach pastor, a singles pastor, a pastor to families, a youth pastor, a children's pastor? The range of titles goes on and on, and each holds a different set of responsibilities.

The kind of pastor you become will be determined by God's design in the gifts and interests he has given you. As David Horner writes, "Our calling is not measured by the plethora of gifts we have received but according to the purposes God has for the unique gifts he has entrusted to each of us."[27] Contrary to popular belief, we don't work our way up an imaginary corporate ladder commencing at children's pastor and culminating as the senior pastor of a megachurch. Angie Ward confirms that "we live in a culture that expects upward progress. And in pastoral ministry, that climb leads to the senior pastorate."[28]

I served part-time as a youth pastor during my seminary training in an ethnic church. Many of the students' parents refused to call me Pastor Matt, because I was not ordained at the time. Therefore, I was not deemed a legitimate pastor. Only ordained ministers were given the respectful title of pastor. In that particular congregation, I was given the made-up title of evangelist. I suspect that in many churches, children's pastors and youth ministers are not given the rightful respect due them since these positions are somehow seen as less praiseworthy than senior ministry positions.

Generalizing here, if preaching, teaching, and vision casting are not your primary skill sets, don't apply for senior pastor positions. If you do not have the gifts of administration and leadership, stay clear from executive pastor openings. You get the picture. It is crucial to match the pastoral position with our unique sets of gifts and talents. God does not call everyone to become a senior pastor or a youth pastor.

27. Horner, *Practical Guide for Life and Ministry*, 27.
28. Ward, "First Chair to Second Fiddle."

On this topic, Angie Ward offers some helpful guidelines. She presents five themes that we can explore as we contemplate which position best suits us:

- *Gifting.* Not everyone called into ministry is gifted for the senior pastor role. Leaders who are gifted more specifically rather than generally, or who have a passion for a certain life stage or type of ministry, will often thrive in a staff setting where they can minister more specifically out of their strengths and passions.

- *Personality.* Similar to the issue of giftedness, some individuals find they do not possess the personality most often associated with the "lead dog" role. Instead, these individuals shun or even avoid the driver's seat, preferring to seat themselves in a supportive role on the bus.

- *Calling.* Some leaders have never even sensed a nudging toward a senior pastor position. Others, however, realize their true calling only after trying unsuccessfully to fill shoes that have been designed for someone else.

- *Contentment.* Everyone, even senior pastors, will find their career trajectory plateauing at some point. "Bigger and better" positions don't keep appearing. Contentment is not found on the next rung of the career ladder.

- *Influence.* While the first chair is typically viewed as the seat with the most influence to create and cast vision, associates can have equal impact in terms of actual influence and day-to-day relationships.[29]

One simple way to evaluate your ministerial role is to consult a pastor or mentor whom you trust and discuss your options. He or she may extend insight concerning your strengths and giftedness for a specific ministry position. Ascertain what role best coincides with your passions, talents, and interests. Engage in conversations with people serving in various capacities to get a flavor of what they do daily. Ask lots of questions. And of course, pray for God's direction.

---

29. Ward, "First Chair to Second Fiddle."

My Testimony of Calling

God calls each person differently. My calling experience, in being dedicated by my mother for pastoral work, is unique. Not everyone is set apart for ministry in this way. Yet the following story reflects how God disclosed his specific calling on my life. As the time arrived for me to go off to college, my mother again reminded me of my calling to become a pastor. However, the thought of becoming a pastor or missionary was still not my ambition or conviction. Feelings of resentment resurfaced. I was steadfast to take full advantage of my newfound freedom and to live like a libertine, free from rules and regulations. Consequently, during my first two years of college I attended parties, drank many weekends, and even took up smoking for a period of time.

I eventually landed on a history major and studied abroad in Oxford, England, during my junior year in the fall of 1997. During that semester overseas, God revealed his calling to full-time ministry in an undeniable way. One afternoon, I took a stroll in one of the university's impeccable gardens when I had an uncontrollable desire to smoke. I had quit for some time, but the itch resurfaced. I went to the local convenience store and bought a pack of overpriced cigarettes. I went back to the garden and started to inhale. Out of the corner of my eye, I saw the rector of the Anglican Church near Oxford University, who happened to take an afternoon saunter at the same time. Startled by his presence, I quickly threw the cigarette down and put it out. At that moment, I felt God asking me, "What are you doing with the second chance I have given you?" I heard the chorus of a Christian worship song repeat over and over again from my youth. The presence of God was undeniable as he revealed my sin and showed me how far I had strayed. I wept as I prayed to God, "Jesus, whatever you want me to do, I will do it!" In that prayer, I personally accepted God's calling to full-time ministry. I always thought my mom was crazy in forecasting my future, but obviously God knows best. And it was his intention all along.

Although ministry remains difficult for me even as a seminary professor, I am grateful to my mother for her prayer of dedication. Who knows what would have happened had my mother not courageously prayed for a miracle? Today, I cannot believe I have the privilege of serving Jesus in full-time Christian ministry. Most likely, your parents did not set you apart for pastoral work, but God has called you in his unique way. Our calling is a personal conviction, tested in Scripture and validated by God's people. We must personally experience God's calling before we make any plans to lead God's church. It's that important. Be certain of your calling. God promises to take care of the rest.

Conclusion

During my time serving as a seminary professor, probably the number one question I get from students regards their calling. Many seminarians are unsure of whether or not they are called to full-time vocational ministry. I get it. I understand the complexity this question raises. How can a person be absolutely certain that he or she is called by God in this way? Isn't there any wiggle room for one's calling being a process or a journey?[30] The short answer is yes. There is no one-size-fits-all calling experience. For some, calling is definite and undeniable like the Apostle Paul's vision on the Damascus Road, while others try to run from a clear sense of call like Jonah's call to preach to the Ninevites. A third group of potential ministers just can't commit because of their lingering questions about their inadequacies, their character, the life of a pastor, or the luxuries their families would have to give up.

To complicate matters, the long answer to this question is also no. Even for those who at one time are confident in God's call, there are moments in every pastoral servant's life where he or she has doubts and experiences rough patches in ministry. You will encounter moments of self-doubt, crisis, trauma, pain, suffering, lament, fatigue, depression, and even burnout. In other seasons, you will experience the greatest joys and highest of highs from unlikely conversions and congregants becoming transformed disciples. Callings can also change. You may be called for a season as a pastor but then pivot to become a full-time missionary, Christian counselor, chaplain, teacher at a Christian school, in my case a seminary professor, or even something else.

Thankfully, we are not alone in this journey called ministry. We take comfort in Jesus' words in John 16:33, "I have told you these things, so that in me you may have peace. In this world you will have trouble. But take heart! I have overcome the world." One caveat to mention here is that if you are uncertain about your calling or have serious reservations even after beginning in the pastorate, please consider taking some time to step away, pray, and consult with others.

30. Padilla, *Now That I'm Called*, 11.

Once you determine your personal calling, you must receive a call from a congregation that matches your new pastoral role. We are not pastors unless we have people to lead. You also can't be a pastor unless a church wants you to be their shepherd. How, then, do you find the right church? That will be the subject of our next lesson.

Ask Yourself

1. Am I certain about my calling, and what criteria will I use to determine its accuracy?

2. What about pastoral ministry excites me, and what do I fear?

3. Which pastoral qualities do I possess?

4. In accordance with those qualities, what pastoral role will I pursue?

2

Find the Right Church

A Matter of Urgency or Prudence

It HAD BEEN A relaxing afternoon as I sat on the couch enjoying a novel when my father-in-law entered the living room. As a surgeon, my father-in-law worked tirelessly to provide for his loved ones. On this day, making his way to the kitchen, he stopped midstride, turned toward me, and asked, "So what's wrong with Connecticut?" What he was referring to was a pastoral ministry position offered to me if I would just take the plunge. Because he is diligent in all things, I can only imagine how much it perplexed him to see his son-in-law lounging on the sofa when he could be exercising his theological training in a church, especially one eager to receive him.

They say that for most pastors the journey to finding the right church is comparable to dating and getting married shortly thereafter. Courting a church can be mystifying, and many experience highs and lows. The outset of my search process wasn't any different. After completing my graduate program overseas, I mentioned to a friend of my pursuit of a full-time ministry position. With my best intentions at heart, he asked for a copy of my resume just in case he heard of promising leads. He soon heard of a church in Connecticut looking for a pastor and dropped my name and resume to this church without my knowledge. After a couple of weeks, I had become this congregation's leading pastoral candidate. It also turned out that my mother-in-law was longtime friends with a prominent elder at that church. So in the minds of various people, I was clearly destined to serve this congregation. This led to my father-in-law's query: "What's wrong with Connecticut?"

For a new pastor, finding the right church is a critical step. It may potentially make or break how we view ministry for the rest of our careers. To be clear, finding the right church doesn't mean that our experiences will be free of problems. No church is perfect, whether big, medium, or small. Likewise, discovering the right church does not require us to serve that church indefinitely. Rather, spotting the right congregation is a matter of being obedient to God and his calling for our lives. It's trusting in the promise that God really does know what's best for us.

For many, it can be enticing to take the first break that comes our way. There comes a point in the waiting period that we can even become desperate. Doug Talley recounts his experience with such a temptation. He writes,

> My first invitation to serve came when we were in seminary and I was looking for ministry experience. I didn't think the church position was the best fit, but I felt like my choices were limited. Against my better judgment, I was about to accept it. My wife was able to convince me that a bad ministry fit does not yield a good experience. . . . I declined the position. . . . Declining that ministry opportunity soon led to my first, and thus far, only pastorate, which has lasted over 19 years.[1]

Pastoral search committees may tell you in a flattering way that you are the solution to their ministerial void. Yet, we can't always believe them. New pastors shouldn't chase after what is urgent; they should rather hand over control to God, who promises to escort us from start to finish. Whether we receive one offer or several, the question every young pastor must ask is "how do I decide on which church to serve?"

This lesson speaks to these matters and will help us contemplate the church's call in light of our calling as pastors. In it, I illustrate personal experiences in the obscure so-called waiting period of being a pastoral candidate. While every person's experience in landing the right church will be unique, there are widespread lessons to be applied. When I began looking for a church to serve, I repeated one prayer to God: "Please make it undeniably clear which church I will serve. I want to obey you." As we explore the possibilities out there, may we be able to say with confidence as David, the psalmist, wrote so long ago, "I waited patiently for the LORD; he inclined to me and heard my cry" (Ps 40:1).

1. Talley, "Listen to Your Spouse," 75.

Define Your Job Description

It was my first pastoral interview process, and I had no idea what to expect. One thing was absolutely clear. I wanted to prepare an engaging, God-exalting sermon. After I preached a message on the humility of Christ from Philippians 2, my wife and I strolled around the sanctuary after the worship service to greet everyone. By their expressions, it seemed that we were well received and that the message resonated favorably. A few minutes went by when one of the elders approached us. We were escorted to the pastor's study. Entering somewhat nervously, we sat down and were given the news that we were offered the position. Although I was fairly relieved, I couldn't believe my ears when I heard "So, Matt, why don't you make a decision today?" My second cousin, who is a pastor on the East Coast, introduced me to this congregation. He and the senior pastor were ministry colleagues and close friends. I went into the weekend visit with the assumption that the church would provide specific details about the job description as well as other pertinent information.

While relatively young and naïve to the process, I was confused by this pastor's determination to hire me. How could either of us make such a monumental decision in the moment? I needed additional information and time for prayer and discernment. So I asked, "What is my job description?" He replied nonchalantly, "You know—the usual pastoral responsibilities." Based on his demeanor, I knew that I wouldn't receive a definitive answer. I thanked him for the opportunity and asked for some additional time to think it over for the sake of seeking God's direction. The pastor agreed to give me two weeks. To my surprise, he called a few days later and wanted my decision. In his mind, I apparently didn't need the full two weeks to wait for God's confirmation. Yet by this time, my wife and I already felt convicted that God had something else in store for us. So we declined.

Whether one is applying for a senior, associate, or assistant pastoral role, the church and the candidate should agree on basic ministerial functions the pastor will fulfill. The job description functions like a nonbinding agreement between the congregation and the pastor. Obviously, we can't possibly quantify the roles that pastors play in the life of a church. My job description more or less evolved during the years that I served my church family. At the time of my interview, however, nothing was set in place.

For instance, as a senior pastor of a small congregation, it's conceivable to have numerous responsibilities. I needed to juggle many tasks, including preaching for two services (one smaller service for ministry servants such as Sunday school teachers); vision casting; leadership training; teaching adult Sunday school, baptism, and membership classes; leading Friday night Bible study/worship (including another weekly sermon or Bible lesson); performing weddings and funerals; facilitating a weekly small group in our home and overseeing the entire small group ministry; leading praise occasionally; participating in short-term mission trips and local outreach; mentoring; carrying out administration; and loving the flock through pastoral care. I'm not exaggerating when I say that it was a lot to handle. Certain responsibilities required attention every week, namely, preaching, teaching, mentoring, administration, and pastoral care. Yet, some of the other demands were less frequent.

At times, we must serve God's people in ways that extend beyond the original job description. Ministry can be messy. For this reason, we should be flexible to make adjustments in our schedule, based on the unpredictable lives of hurting, complex people. As an example, the work of a pastor may involve participating in charitable or controversial events in our local communities. We may need to make recurring visits to the hospital where someone is unwell or nearing death. God may prompt us to undertake a weekly visit to the county prison when a church member has committed a serious crime and is in desperate need of our encouragement and prayer. Our pastoral service may require counseling a married couple on the brink of divorce.

Our job descriptions are malleable, but they provide a conduit for our own sanity and effectiveness. By knowing what the leaders and church members expect of us, we can customize our time so that we can concentrate on our God-given responsibilities and steer away from seemingly pressing matters that are actually not. That's why it is crucial for all pastors to have a clear sense of what the church expects from us, and vice versa.

Stick to Your Convictions

Another church that we visited seemed, at first, to be an ideal situation. The position was to be the senior pastor of a multiracial, multigenerational church on the West Coast. George Yancey defines multiracial churches as ones where "no one racial group makes up more than 80 percent of the attendees of at least one of the major worship services."[2] Although not exactly multiracial by this definition, this church was diverse in that the membership comprised

2. Yancey, *One Body One Spirit*, 15.

Americans of Caucasian, Hispanic, and Asian origins. Predominantly Asian American in heritage, the ethnic groups of parishioners included Japanese, Chinese, Koreans, Filipinos, and Vietnamese, among others. Second, the congregants were multigenerational, including recent immigrants all the way to fourth- and fifth-generation Americans. For these reasons, this varied ethnic and generational demographic was appealing.

I received a phone call from an elder of the church. The inflection in his voice depicted enthusiasm, and he asked for a resume and sermon recording. He had found my profile on a seminary website that placed alumni in different ministries. During our phone conversation, he asked tough questions concerning my theological perspectives and my philosophy of ministry. After several days, I received an invitation to visit the church as a pastoral candidate. There was one major glitch, however. The elder strongly disagreed with my stance on women's roles in ministry. He called himself a "soft complementarian," which meant women were prohibited in his mind from serving the church as a pastor or elder. I, on the other hand, described myself as an egalitarian, arguing that God calls both men and women to serve him in the pastoral office and in eldership. We exchanged several emails on this topic. I presented what I perceived to be cogent scriptural evidence for my beliefs, as did he. Nothing was resolved for the time being.

The weekend visit to the church went well. The members were affectionate and inviting. At the end of our time there, we found out that the elder, whom I had been in contact with all along, was the only elder of the church. In one later email, he confidently exclaimed, "I am the chosen elder of God's church," which meant he had the lone voice and vote for every area of church governance. Immediately, we knew that this was not a healthy congregation. Before our departure at our visit, the elder took me aside and explained that the church would hire me only if I abandoned my position on women in ministry. My brain triggered a conversation where my seminary mentor shared how every church has at least one bully. That weekend, I met the bully face to face. The irony is that several godly females established this church. Many in the church valued women's roles in ministry and hoped that the next pastor would similarly validate females' contributions to every facet of church life.

Over the next few weeks, the elder and I continued to swap emails. I stood my ground and told him I wouldn't alter my view. Then he made the searing comment that I did not uphold the authority of Scripture and that my position would also make me susceptible to embracing homosexuality as a biblical value. I was offended. So I made my thoughts known to him as well. I challenged him on being the only elder at the church. I expressed concern that his usurping of power was in all likelihood destroying God's church. Providentially, some congregants heard about what happened between us. The elder eventually left the church. While I have not kept in contact with this church, I still pray for their unity and spiritual health.

As you have probably guessed, we did not accept this church's call either. However, we learned a valuable lesson. A new pastor should stick to his or her convictions. While the topic of women in ministry is what many would consider to be a nonessential subject, these kinds of topics can split a church and its members. Such differences caused denominations to form in the first place. As new pastors, we must stand firm on essential matters of faith and doctrine, such as the divinity of Christ and the exclusivity of Jesus as the only way to eternal life in a pluralistic society. We must cling to the belief that God is one in three persons, Father, Son, and Holy Spirit, and be willing to defend other central truths.

At the same time, however, nonessentials have the potential to become essential. Human beings are often stubborn and prideful. Unfortunately, pastors fall into this category as well. On this particular occasion, neither the elder nor I was willing to compromise. One might say that I should've been more flexible. However, since we were both adamant, this topic would have sparked division throughout the church. And at some point in the future, one of us would've been pushed out involuntarily.

It is convenient for beginning pastors to check our theological and ministerial convictions at the entrance of the church and oblige members along the way. For pastors, the temptation towards people pleasing is palpable. Charles Stone makes this confession, "I now realize that instead of being driven primarily to please God by a vision he gave me, I easily acquiesced to do what pleased people. Although I never compromised my theology or my morals, I would try to please others and avoid criticism at all costs."[3] Indeed, God desires unity in the church. There are moments in a pastor's life when he must yield on certain positions in order to unify God's family. Ministry is not about us or our ideas and best practices. We may lose the battle in order to win the war of preserving our church members. However, if we know prior to entering a pastorate that either theological or ministerial philosophies do not align with a potential congregation, we must take that disagreement seriously. It is naïve to think that our simple love for the

3. Stone, *People-Pleasing Pastors*, 14.

flock will cover any biblical, theological disagreements that we have with confrontational parishioners or lay leaders.

I encourage you to openly share your biblical, theological, practical, ministry-oriented beliefs during the search process rather than conceal them. For example, if you hold the position that children should not participate in Communion, do not tell the pastoral search committee that you're willing to open the Lord's table to everyone because that has been the church's practice. If you insist that giving to mission work should represent a certain portion of the church's budget, speak up and say so. Be willing to discuss dissimilar perspectives when they arise. Be up-front with the church and stick to your convictions. Don't stretch or alter your positions just because you think it will get you the offer. Obviously, we may never agree with the church on every single matter. That's normative. Yet be careful not to compromise your convictions and beliefs. When we honor the office of pastor by being candid, it is only natural that the right church will come our way.

Beware of False Advertising

Southern California is a popular destination not just for the rich and famous but also for fledgling pastors seeking the illusory pathway to ministry success. Some of the most influential pastors and churches today inhabit this part of the country. Born and raised in Chicago, I have often felt a strong gravitational pull toward California. During my search for a pastoral position, I once stumbled across a ministry posting in a Los Angeles suburb. Since my sister-in-law lived nearby, my wife saw this ministry as an opportunity to reunite with her family. On paper, it was a perfect fit.

On the morning of our visit, I was asked at the last minute to preach for the youth group because I was told these students would eventually join our congregation. I was happy to accommodate them. When that service concluded, it was time to preach for the young adults. The mood was ambivalent since the current pastor of young adults was also in attendance. There were about fifty people scattered throughout the sanctuary. Some of the members appeared eager to worship God, while you could tell that others had "better" things to do. After lunch, the young adults asked us to share our life stories and our ministry vision for the future. I greatly enjoyed our discussion, and the prospect of serving this church became more appealing.

However, when I was called in to meet with the senior pastor, the once-promising situation turned south rather quickly. As I took a seat, he smiled and introduced himself as *the* pastor of the church. He disclosed how he was a former vice president of a leading manufacturing company and that God had called him to full-time parish ministry. I admired him for his obedience and sacrifice.

He asked me how the weekend was going. I acknowledged my initial enthusiasm about the church. He smirked for a split second, and then he laid down the law. He declared that I should mentally discard my doctoral degree and that it meant nothing to him. I was to be a servant of Christ and not a doctor of philosophy. He said, "As long as you remember that and do your job, you can have the position." Fair enough. I understood that my additional theological training had nothing directly to do with being a pastor, but the way he approached the topic seemed defensive and exposed his insecurity. He extended an offer and gave me a deadline of a week to make my decision.

Being a conflict-averse personality, my heart fluttered as I felt compelled to ask about the salary package. With a sense of unease, I probed him. Surprised by my courage, he responded, "We will give you $3,000 per month total." My jaw dropped. The church advertised an annual compensation package of $48,000 to $55,000, including other pastoral benefits. Since this was an associate position, I suppose my first inclination should have been gratitude. However, the point is, what was offered was significantly less than the sticker price, and we are talking about living in Southern California.

It was only fair to bring up the discrepancy. "Pastor, the position called for a compensation package between $48,000 to $55,000 and additional benefits," I commented. Noticing my troubled demeanor, he continued: "If you and your wife need additional support it could be offered, when necessary." I felt blatantly manipulated. And what came next outraged me. The pastor said, "What are you complaining about? I receive $29,000 from the church, so you should be more than appreciative."

Be assured, new pastor, that not every church is stingy at the pastor's expense. However, the local church is made up of sinners just like you and me. In Romans 3:23, Paul says it best: "For there is no distinction, since all have sinned and fall short of the glory of God." Some congregations take advantage of novice ministers whether they intend to or not. They may attempt to get away with thriftiness rather than modeling God's generosity. So beware of false advertising. The deceitfulness can be masked. Perhaps you will be offered a parsonage in shambles, although you were led to believe it was recently renovated. Maybe the church will extend a certain number of vacation weeks that you or your family may never get to enjoy. Some congregations expect the spouse of the pastor to work just as diligently as their employee without gratitude or compensation. We may find ourselves serving a church that is in financial crisis, and we're not certain where our salary will come from the following year.

Oftentimes, neither the church nor the candidate is openly willing to reveal flaws because of fear of rejection. This is only human. As a general rule of thumb, try to get certain promises made by the church in writing for the sake of mutual accountability, particularly when they deal with salary and retirement packages, insurance (e.g., medical, dental, vision, disability, or life), housing allowances, vacations, and continuing education. We can be up-front about the general needs of our family. We can seek wise counsel about the cost of living in that region. Once we relocate, it's difficult to turn the moving van around. Get the facts straight prior to making your decision, even if it means showing courage. And try to keep your integrity by staying faithful to the promises you make, whether they are reciprocated or not. God will honor our authenticity, and churches will respect us for it. That communal trust will go a long way, especially as we launch our ministries.

Be Flexible with Location

In Luke 10:2, Jesus said to his disciples, "The harvest is plentiful, but the laborers are few; therefore ask the Lord of the harvest to send out laborers into his harvest." From the first century until now, the global church has always needed full-time servants. While some obey God's call and go where he asks, others will only yield when the asphalt is paved and smooth. Adair Lummis reports that in churches with an active membership of more than 200, "lay leaders are typically quite discriminating in choosing a pastor. Search committees have more resources at their disposal and more support in using them."[4] On the flip side, many rural and smaller churches can't afford to be overly selective. For churches located in less appealing regions, it can be extremely challenging to attract qualified ministers.[5]

Some common temptations for new pastors are to follow money, weather, and a large flock. In today's consumer mentality, pastors and parishioners alike can chase riches and comfort. However, Jesus calls us to

4. Lummis, "What Do Lay People?," 6.

5. See Witmer, *Big Gospel in Small Places.*

radical obedience.[6] Are we going to travel where God leads us or seek self-ish aspirations? The writer of Proverbs 20:24 got it right when he said, "A person's steps are directed by the LORD. How then can anyone understand their own way?" Along the same lines, Jeffrey Miller writes, "When we ma-nipulate our own life against the will of God, we leave a trail of damage in our path. Controlling or forcing our agenda or timing will ultimately prove harmful."[7] While humans seek to control life at every turn, God knows us better than we know ourselves. He has the right ministry place in mind, if only we can trust him. Through visiting many churches and meeting various pastoral search committees, God eventually led us to the right church. But I can't say that I was initially pleased with the location.

It had been six months since I intentionally started the pastoral search process. I had already interviewed with eight different churches all over the United States. Each of them said yes except for one search com-mittee that wanted more ministry experience. But, we still knew the right church hadn't come. Already into June, I was getting a bit worried. I had heard from friends in the ministry that many church positions begin in the fall. I felt like time was running out. A range of thoughts entered my mind. Am I just being too picky? Am I taking matters into my own hands? What if I already missed the church God had planned for me? The only thing I could do was continue searching.

My sister-in-law asked if we had seen any ministry opportunities in Colorado. To that point, we hadn't seen any listings. She shared how many of her friends in California were relocating to Colorado because of its affordability and pleasant climate. I apologize to Coloradans and my former church members, but I associated Denver with Nazareth. "Could anything good come from there?" Denver wasn't on the radar. It wasn't part of my plan.

I went to a familiar website that listed new ministry positions avail-able in the United States and abroad. That day, something providential happened. A job posting appeared for a senior pastor position in Colo-rado. Despite my disbelief, I thought it couldn't hurt to send in a resume and a sermon. What's the worst that could happen? To make a long story short, God had a clear road map for us, orchestrating his plan all along. After several telephone interviews, we were invited for a formal visit. My initial prediction seemed correct. As the plane swooped down on Denver

6. See Platt, *Follow Him*.

7. Miller, *Hazards of Being a Man*, 39.

International Airport, I saw nothing but flat, open space. I was right. There's nothing good here.

After a weekend full of meetings, preaching, and making initial contacts with the people in the church, my wife and I spent some time debriefing. "Was there anything that you found noticeably wrong or disturbing?" I asked. "No," she replied. "How about you?" I wanted to respond with a booming, "Yes, there was something terribly wrong," but my heart sensed absolute peace about the church. As mentioned earlier, I had been praying the entire weekend: "Heavenly Father, please make it undeniably clear to me which church I will serve. Help me to follow your call."

Shortly, it became unmistakable that we had finally found the church God had prepared for us. The vision and theological beliefs of the church aligned with our own. We were offered a salary and compensation package that was sufficient for our financial needs. The church owned a spacious parsonage for us to begin a family. And the congregation ultimately voted us in with 95 percent approval. There was nothing standing in our way. Even though Colorado was not our first choice in location, we recognized that God had specially arranged this place for us. The only thing I could do was to trust, obey, and find out what this church and I were made of.

We can search long and hard, but there is no perfect church out there. Every congregation has strengths and challenges. I encountered my share of triumphs and surprises in that pastorate. And over those years, we received confirmation time and time again of God's call to that community. One of the most difficult things to do as a new pastor or any Christian for that matter is to trust God completely. As a result of this process, I made Proverbs 3:5–6 my new "life verses": "Trust in the LORD with all your heart and lean not on your own understanding; in all your ways submit to him, and he will make your paths straight." God is sovereign and knows what we can and cannot handle. God will direct our steps one foot after the other. Trust him.

The Candidate Process

Beyond these difficult lessons learned, other considerations may sharpen our thinking as we attempt to pinpoint our first congregation to serve. What can we do to best prepare ourselves for this important calling? The first thing we should do is learn how the process works.

Take Advantage of Staffing Websites

If you belong to a denomination that simply places candidates in unoccupied pastorates, begin by asking your regional directors what to do. They will have specific protocol for you to follow. For those who are not assigned to a congregation, the process of finding the right church typically begins when we find a ministry opening that appeals to our interests and gifts. Many websites list vacancies in all sorts of pastorates both domestic and foreign.

Especially for those who come from nondenominational backgrounds (a significant number), a good starting place might be the website of a seminary nearby or the seminary from which you graduated. As an example, Gordon-Conwell Theological Seminary in South Hamilton, Massachusetts, offers a site called ministrylist.com that advertises ministry opportunities and enables seminary alumni to post their qualifications so that potential churches can pursue them. Other websites allow candidates to view databases of pastoral positions and also place resumes on the website for churches to peruse. Take advantage of this technology, and get your name out there.

Items Churches Require

Once we have found a church that intrigues us, it is appropriate only to send in the items they request. Usually, a church will ask for a cover letter stating your interest in the position, how you heard of the opening, and why you would make a successful candidate. Spend quality time on drafting the cover letter. Learn about their congregation and denomination via their website. Only share relevant information about yourself and your qualifications. Don't be excessive about why you believe you make the perfect candidate. And check for spelling and grammatical errors. If you can, get a friend who is gifted in proofreading to read through it.

Second, it is advantageous to attach a current resume (shorter, one to two pages) or Curriculum Vitae (full length CV, usually without page restrictions) that highlights your educational background, your ministry and work experiences, relevant skills, and names and contact information of personal references. In this resume or CV, focus on your strengths and don't be ashamed to point out your God-given abilities. We can be confident without being conceited.

With regard to personal references, show courtesy by asking your references for permission prior to listing them. Also, be certain that this individual knows you well enough to speak about your aptitude for ministry. A common gaffe that many seminarians and new pastors make is to ask a professor or former pastor for a letter of reference simply because they received an A in her class or because the pastor is somewhat acquainted with you. This happens all too frequently in the seminary context, where I receive an email request to serve as a reference. Oftentimes, I barely know the individual. To the person's chagrin, I usually turn down such requests.

The person who provides a reference should know you on a personal level, and should have spent a good measure of time with you, therefore being able to comment on your Christian character, your spiritual life, your family life, your ability to work with others, your depth of knowledge and integration of theology and Bible, and not just about your academic competence and unsubstantiated potential for ministry. In other words, they should be able to comment easily about your strengths and weaknesses and not sit there and have to scratch their heads wondering about how to answer these questions about you.

In addition, some churches may ask for your statement of faith (i.e., what you believe about theology), your philosophy of ministry (i.e., how you view the purpose of the church and your role in it), your philosophy of leadership (i.e., your vision of leadership or style of leadership), and sometimes even position papers (i.e., your view on a particular theological or ministry-related issue that is substantiated with Scripture). You probably wrote some of these ideas down in a systematic theology or practical ministry paper in seminary. It will help you to reflect on these matters prior to the interview. You don't want to be ill-prepared.

Last, especially for lead/senior pastor or teaching pastor positions, the church will request an audio or video sermon or two that you have preached. If you are currently in training at a seminary and have opportunities to preach, try to record your messages. They will come in handy later. I learned this lesson the hard way. During my time as a part-time youth pastor, I didn't record a single sermon even though I preached weekly for two years (over 100 sermons). By the time I began looking for a full-time ministry position, I hadn't recorded a single message that I could share with prospective churches. By God's grace, a friend asked me to speak at his church's retreat, which presented an occasion to record several messages. I sent in two sermons from the weekend. Don't be caught off guard. Be prepared in advance. Have every sermon recorded when you get the opportunity. It will be well worth the effort.

Get Ready for the Phone/Video Interviews and Formal Visit

If the pastoral search committee views your application positively, they will set up phone or video interviews. In every church where I was a candidate, I first went through a series of phone interviews. The purpose of the phone/video interview is for the church to get to know you better, and vice versa. It is really an opportunity for the committee to minimize financial resources and assess you as a potential pastor without incurring the cost of flying you out. During these initial conversations, the church will ask you further about who you are as a person and as a future pastor. They will ask you about your family and your personal interests. They will ask you about your previous experiences in ministry, if applicable. They may ask questions about situational ethics and how you might handle certain behavioral conflicts in the church. They might probe you on your positions on difficult topics like abortion, in vitro fertilization, human sexuality, or women's roles in ministry, among others. They may even want to know your vision for this particular ministry and your five-year plan for them as a church. Be ready for anything and everything.

If the committee senses a need to progress with you, they will invite you for a formal interview and visit. What comes next? If you are married, one consideration that is frequently overlooked is whether the church can afford to bring you and your spouse on the trip. With such a critical decision to be made, it is worthwhile to ask if your spouse can accompany you. You want him or her to also be familiar with the church, the location, and the congregants. If this is not feasible, then you will have to make the best decision that you possibly can under the circumstances.

Your formal visit and interview comprise several elements. First, make sure you have a solid, field-tested message or two to preach (even for non-senior pastor positions). The church will want to get a sense of you in the pulpit in a "live" setting and see how the congregation responds to your preaching content and style. Don't be surprised if you are asked to preach more than once over the weekend. In several churches, I was asked to preach more than once to different age groups. Try to remember that you are there to serve and not to be served.

The visit may also include various lunch or dinner meetings with current staff, the pastoral search committee, and other lay leaders. Try to relax and get to know them. Be yourself. But keep this in mind: They are not just interviewing you. You are interviewing them as well. You want to make sure that you leave no unanswered questions regarding the church, the position, the surrounding location, the quality of schools in the area, the job responsibilities, the compensation package, and any other information you need to make a sensible decision.

Leonora Tubbs Tisdale suggests exploring the church's archival resources, such as committee meeting minutes, Sunday worship bulletins, financial records, letters from the denomination, and church newsletters.[8] Today, it might even help to read through the outgoing pastor's blog or listen to a podcast to see what he or she might express about past issues facing the congregation. In addition, Angie Best-Boss raises some thoughtful questions to ask concerning the church, including:

- What impact does the church have, or want to have, on the community?

- What does the congregation want in a pastor?

- What is the church's current financial state (i.e., amount of debt, in reserve)?

- Why is there a need for a pastoral transition?

- What is the current average attendance?

- Describe the congregation (i.e., demographics, involvement, personality).[9]

Finally, the formal visit may present an opportunity to become familiar with the area. The members of the congregation will want you to be enthusiastic about your new surroundings before decisions are rendered. They may try to spice up your visit. It is helpful to bring appropriate clothing for recreation. Be prepared to go skiing or surfing depending on the region. On one occasion, some of the church members invited me to play tennis and later swim at an outdoor recreation facility. You may also want to bring some more formal attire in case they take you out for a meal at a popular local eatery. If the weekend is going well, they might even take

---

8. Tisdale, *Preaching as Local Theology*, 69–70.

9. Best-Boss, *Surviving Your First Year*, 5.

you to the church parsonage for a viewing or visit other housing options. Let this be your opportunity to get a feel for the town. Ask questions in the process. And within boundaries, remember to have fun.

Decision Time

In the coming weeks, the church may or may not offer you a position. Generally speaking, many congregations' bylaws stipulate that they cannot vote for at least one or two weeks after the final candidate's visit. Sometimes, they will interview on site one, two, or even three potential candidates before naming a final candidate. You may even be asked to come back a second or third time. Remember, this is a very important decision for the church as it is for you and your family (if applicable). While it's easy to do so, try not to get overly stressed out during this period of waiting. Do your part by seeking God in prayer. Continue to find out as much as you can about the church. Think through whether or not your passions and ministry gifts align with the job description. In moments of desperation, we may say yes to the wrong church or to the wrong pastoral role. Ask the Holy Spirit whether this is the right place for you and your family to serve. After the church has voted, you will be notified of the result, whether it's favorable or not.

Trust in God's Sovereignty

When a congregation invites you to become its next pastor, it doesn't mean you have to accept. An open door is not sufficient evidence that we are to walk through it. It sounds crazy to turn down a ministry opportunity. But, you need to be sure if you're going to say yes. Before my first son, Ryan, was born, my wife and I participated in a four-week birthing class to prepare for the imminent labor and delivery. During the final class, our instructor handed out several note cards with medical procedures written on them. We were told to set aside what she called a list of nonnegotiables, meaning the elements of labor and delivery that were most important to us. It turns out that during Sarah's labor the nurses ended up utilizing almost all the medical procedures that we didn't want, but those few nonnegotiables were preserved. I would encourage those who are looking for a pastoral position to write down a similar list of nonnegotiables. What five to ten elements are most important to you in finding the right church? Write these down as you pray and submit to God's will. In some cases, these nonnegotiable components will aid you in the discernment process.

Most importantly, prayer is essential in our decision making. Oftentimes, we claim to believe in the sovereignty of God but fail to practice this truth in daily life. As ministers of the gospel, we help ourselves when we have faith that God knows what he is doing with our lives. God understands the needs of his church as well as our abilities. God will not send us to a church where we cannot handle the responsibilities and the pressures. Pray that God will lead you to the right place and the best church for you and your family to exercise your gifts. Remember that God is a loving, gracious, and faithful father who cares deeply for us and for his flock. When you have prayed diligently, God will give you the peace and boldness that are necessary to take the next leap of faith. You can say "yes" to the right church and "no, thank you" to the one God has impeded. Be faithful to God by heeding his call wherever and whenever he leads you.

Ask Yourself

1. What are the most important factors for me (and my spouse) in finding the right church?

2. What questions about the church and about the position will I ask during the interview process?

3. Do I have a realistic job description in place?

4. What are my nonnegotiables?

3

Acclimate to the Pastor's Life

What Pastors Do

ON MY FIRST DAY as pastor, I set up my home office at the church parsonage. Being a type A personality, I quickly unpacked my two dozen boxes of books and placed them on newly assembled bookshelves. Later, I covered a bare wall with my diplomas, a calendar, and a small bronze plaque given to me by my mother, inscribed with Psalm 18:2, which reads: "The LORD is my rock, my fortress and my deliverer; my God is my rock, in whom I take refuge, my shield and the horn of my salvation, my stronghold." These were the very words I needed daily. After organizing the room to my satisfaction, I sat at my desk raring to go, but where was I headed? What came next on the pastoral ministry agenda? I had absolutely no clue.[1]

There is an initial shock in becoming a full-fledged pastor. Nothing can prepare us completely for what our lives will be like. This lesson intends to familiarize us with what life in ministry is like for new ministers. We will not only explore some basic expectations that our parishioners have for us but also anticipate some ministry responsibilities as God's shepherds. We begin our discussion with the sometimes murky transition between life as a seminarian and the life as a pastor in the church. How does life as a student preparing for the ministry differ from ministering to real people?

1. See Alston, Jr., "What a Minister," 250.

From Seminary to the Pastorate

Life in seminary is quite disparate from serving people in a congregation. Seminary classes on pastoral ministry scratched the surface of what pastors do, but they didn't, or more accurately couldn't, give us a comprehensive picture.[2] In seminary, we are given basic tools for ministry: original languages, biblical exegesis, hermeneutics, theology, church history, counseling, leadership, preaching, and so on. Yet Angie Best-Boss observes a profound difference between seminary life and the pastorate: "While seminary focuses on academics, the pastorate is focused on your people."[3] She's right. While there is a certain cadence to the life of a seminary student, our people will throw a wrench into our schedules. Hopefully we will see these "intrusions" or "interruptions" in a positive light.

L. Gregory and Susan Jones argue that "better bridges need to be built between the experience of seminary and the realities of full-time ministry."[4] In seminary, future ministers float ideas around concerning what parish life is like, but they don't have the practical ideas about what it actually involves. This was my experience as a student, and I would assume that I wasn't alone. Similarly, seminarians today tend to live in an imaginary, idealistic world where they enjoy hearing about the romanticized aspects of ministry and don't want to hear about the challenges. For this reason, I try to balance stories about the joys and hardships of pastoral life. If we are ill-prepared for the taxing aspects of ministry, we will be blindsided and may experience early onset burnout. The late Dean Hoge and Jacqueline Wenger found that clergy burnout persists partly because "seminaries should do more to prepare their students for the practical aspects of ministry."[5] In other words, we need to prepare students not just for the public side of ministry of preaching and teaching but also for the nitty-gritty "people" aspect of ministry.

Hanging out with books, for most seminarians, is the easy part. Dealing with the range of personality types in a given congregation is a different story. The fundamental snag, as Wallace Alston, Jr. notes, is that

2. Since the first edition of *7 Lessons for New Pastors* was released, others have written on the topic as well, including Helopoulos, *The New Pastor's Handbook*; Hughes, *The Pastor's Book*; Millican and Woodyard, eds., *Before We Forget*; and Wingard, *Help for the New Pastor*.

3. Best-Boss, *Surviving Your First Year*, xii–xiii.

4. Jones and Jones, "Leadership," 17.

5. Hoge and Wenger, *Pastors in Transition*, 202.

there is an "absence of people on their faculties who have firsthand knowledge of pastoral ministry."[6] As a quick aside, even if you earn a PhD in biblical studies or theology with hopes of a full-time teaching position,[7] I strongly encourage you to serve as a full-time pastor first. There are many faculty members in Bible colleges and seminaries who lack full-time pastoral experience. We want to be able to teach our students to integrate head knowledge with practical knowledge of ministering to people. Pastoral ministry is invaluable for a Bible college/seminary professor. While the Joneses correctly maintain that "much of what needs to be learned about pastoral ministry can only be learned in the practice of pastoral ministry,"[8] we can still enter the world of ministry with foreknowledge and insight regarding our new ministerial roles. Why don't we consider initially what our congregants might expect from us?

Expectations of New Pastors

Churches have always had lofty expectations for their current and future pastors, as they should. We want pastors who are competent, people of character, loving, and godly. Duke University Divinity School's Pulpit and Pew Research Project describes several other qualities that the average church is looking for in a pastoral candidate. Adair Lummis outlines nine formative qualities laity hope for in their future pastor:

1. The pastor should have demonstrated competence and religious authenticity for parish ministry.

2. The pastor should be a good preacher and leader of worship.

3. He or she must be a strong spiritual leader for the congregation.

4. The pastor should exemplify commitment to the parish ministry and exhibit ability to maintain boundaries.

5. He or she should be available, approachable, and a warm pastor with good "people skills."

6. Lay members will take into consideration the gender, race, marital status, and sexual orientation of the clergy person.

6. Alston, Jr., "What a Minister," 251.

7. See Gupta, *Prepare, Succeed, Advance.*

8. Jones and Jones, "Leadership," 17.

7. We will consult his or her experience and job tenure in previous positions.

8. The pastor should be a consensus builder, lay ministry coach, and responsive leader.

9. And he or she should be an entrepreneurial evangelist, innovator, and transformational leader.[9]

Quickly surveying this list of pastoral qualities, each is crucial for today's pastor. For the most part, this is what seminaries train pastors to be and to do. We are called to preach and teach the word of God with acumen and display sensitivity to our respective church cultures. We are expected to be relational and muster the patience to listen to the joys and heartaches of people. Pastors are called to demonstrate Spirit-led leadership while modeling servant-like behavior. At the same time, however, if one removes the religious jargon, this list of traits also resembles a job posting for the chief executive officer of a major corporation. It can be stressful to find out later that the pastoral search committee presumes we will embody most, if not all, of these attributes and skills. In one person, it's quite difficult to find the unique skill sets of being a gifted leader, visionary, preacher, teacher, who is also personable, relational, a counselor, and a caregiver. Most people are either task-oriented or people-oriented. Not both.

Truthfully, many members of the laity do not grasp what pastors do on a daily basis. Derek Prime and Alistair Begg explain, "At one extreme some may think we only work on a Sunday, and at the other we may be expected to be able to do everything that needs to be done in the church."[10] Their observation is accurate. On one hand, some congregants approached me and said, "Matt, it must be nice to be paid a full-time salary and watch your sons every day." At the other extreme, one ministry posting for a senior pastor position listed twenty-eight bullet points for their next pastor's qualifications and duties. What was clearly communicated to a candidate reading this advertisement is that this church expects their new minister to fulfill three positions in one. Many new pastors seeking senior positions are also presented with the reality that they have insufficient experience to qualify for senior pastorates. In fact, during my pursuit of a lead minister position, one church explained that it would only consider pastors with at least eight years of full-time senior pastor experience. With such towering

9. Lummis, "What Do Lay People?"
10. Prime and Begg, *On Being a Pastor*, 293.

demands in place, we tease that certain churches hope Jesus Christ will return and be their next senior pastor.

As you look for a church to serve, you may have experienced the same unsettling feeling. When we don't measure up on paper, we question God's calling in our lives. Am I really meant to do this? How can I possibly meet these preconditions or fulfill all these ministerial functions? I'm not super human. I can't be Superman or Superwoman.[11] To some extent, it would help us if parishioners understood that pastors are mortal and get fatigued. We can only do so much. Similarly, we are reminded that God never promises pastors a cushy life. We are called to follow Jesus' model and be servants first, not seeking to be served.

Thus the expectations that pastors and congregants have for each other should exhibit mutual consideration and grace. We need to find a happy medium. There is little wonder why such high levels of burnout, dissatisfaction, and turnover exist among today's young ministers and veterans alike. As beginning pastors, we can innocently enter full-time ministry without comprehending what it entails and encounter members who too quickly place pastors on a pedestal only to be disappointed by their humanity.

But no one said that it has to be this way. That is the good news. A balanced perspective is necessary for clergy and congregation alike. As a word of encouragement, while expectations often remain high for pastors, there are churches willing to take a risk on the right person as well as churches that endorse balance in a pastor's life. Other trailblazers have testified to this certainty. Balance is achievable when we have a lucid job description.

Follow Your Job Description Closely

One of the reasons why a comprehensive job description is so vital for a new pastor is because it provides a blueprint for how we will use our time. The tendency for new pastors is simply to do what we enjoy and forsake the rest. For example, Ronald Sisk explains,

> You're just beginning your pastor-ate [sic]. It's not sermon-preparation day. You can do anything you like. The day stretches before you. If you had your preference of all the possible ministerial tasks you might undertake today, what would you most likely choose to do? That lack of a prescribed routine, it seems to me, is precisely

11. Kim, *Little Book for New Preachers*, 110.

the challenge. Because nobody tells us most of the time what we have to do, most of us tend to do first the things we want to do.[12]

However, if we have a schedule mutually agreed on, we can break down our weeks into units of time. We can set aside a certain number of hours for each ministerial task and for indispensable time spent with our parishioners. We can set up parameters for our own well-being. Boundaries will be put in place so that frustration will be alleviated.

Take a look at the figure below as a sample of how we can break up each day during a given week. This was a typical work week for me as a senior pastor. Of course, depending on your title, your responsibilities will look different. No two weeks will be identical. Ministry requires flexibility and not rigidity to predetermined schedules. Whenever possible, try to work only two out of three time blocks per day. You may want to schedule some pastoral visits during meal times since most people work during regular business hours. In other words, take them out for breakfast or lunch near their workplace. This sample schedule is but one example of a (solo) senior pastor's life. You'll need to incorporate in your schedule daily time spent with our Triune God through Scripture reading and prayer (depending on what works for you). If you are a solo pastor, you should not expect to work a traditional forty-hour week. It will likely be at least fifty hours per week. The shaded areas indicate the time blocks when you'll be formally working. I will share more on the topic of boundaries and balance in the next lesson.

12. Sisk, *Competent Pastor*, 26.

Sample Weekly Schedule

Day	Sunday	Monday	Tuesday	Wednes-day	Thursday	Friday	Saturday
Breakfast (7-8:30)	Go over Sermon	Sabbath	Exercise			Exercise	Prayer Meeting
Morning (9-12)	Worship Service(s)	Sabbath	Staff Meeting/ Admin	Sunday Sermon Prep	Sunday Sermon Prep	Sunday Sermon Prep (Finish)	Leader-ship Meeting
Lunch (12-1:30)	At Church	Sabbath	Visit Member	At Home	Visit Member	At Home	At Home
After-noon (1:30-5)	Church Meetings	Sabbath	Sunday Sermon Prep	SG Bible Study Prep	Rest	Prep for Friday Night Sermon/ Bible Study	Final Admin (1-2 hours) and Rest
Dinner (5-7)	At Home	Sabbath	Ladies' Small Group (SG) at Parson-age (with Sarah)	Dinner with Men's SG at Parsonage	Dinner with Church Members	At Home	At Home
Evening (7-9:30)	Evening with Family	Sabbath	Ladies' SG at Parson-age (with Sarah)	Men's SG at Parsonage	Evening with Church Mem-bers at Parsonage	Friday Night Bible Study/ Worship	Evening with Family

A friend once joined the pastoral staff of a large congregation. Before he accepted this new role, I reminded him to establish his job description. Based on our conversations, he hadn't done so, and he was responsible for exceedingly more than his title warranted. Although it was personally fulfilling in different ways, he filled a void in nearly every facet of church life. As a result, he didn't have much quality time with his wife, nor did he have extended periods to rest. Sadly, his time at the church ended in ministry burnout. Don't take this advice too casually. Have a written job description in hand before commencing your new pastoral role. You won't regret it.

So what do pastors do? To be honest, every pastorate is one of a kind and will require different pastoral responsibilities. What I will try to show in the remaining portions of this lesson is that every minister can welcome and put into practice some overarching principles. Regardless of our ministry title, the first thing is that all pastors are shepherds. An initial way to get acclimated to the pastor's life is to embrace our calling as one who cares for the flock.

The Pastor as Shepherd

Understanding our job description as a shepherd enables us to set the right priorities. Ronald Allen testifies that "our terms *pastoral* and *pastor* derive from a root that means 'shepherd.' The work of a shepherd is a pattern for pastoral work in the congregation."[13] What is a shepherd?

We learn what a shepherd is by exploring what shepherds do. The Old Testament prophet Ezekiel underscores several important traits concerning God, who is the good and faithful shepherd. At the outset, a shepherd is not self-interested but rather cares sincerely for the flock (Ezek 34:2–3). It is easy to become self-interested as a pastor. It's also tempting for new ministers to see their first pastoral call as a stepping-stone to something grander. But God calls us to love our sheep, which requires sacrifice.

How are shepherds instructed to care for the sheep? In this passage, God communicates to Ezekiel the areas where the shepherds of Israel have failed. We're expected to carry out the opposite. God says, "You have not strengthened the weak or healed the sick or bound up the injured. You have not brought back the strays or searched for the lost. You have ruled them harshly and brutally. So they were scattered because there was no shepherd, and when they were scattered they became food for all the wild animals" (Ezek 34:4–5). The implications for pastors are clear. Shepherds visit the sick and strengthen weak and unwell persons (physically and spiritually). They reach out to members who don't come to service. They pursue those who are lost or have exited the church's doors. Shepherds lead in a gentle fashion. And they equip the flock so that they can defend themselves against the enemy's attacks.

In the New Testament, Jesus took the image of pastor as shepherd one giant leap further. Specifically, in John 10:15, he says "and I lay down my life for the sheep." Shepherds care for their sheep even to the point of figurative

13. Allen, *Preaching and Practical Ministry*, 48.

41

and perhaps literal death. That's a sobering thought. As a pastor, I failed numerous times to fully embody the shepherd's call with my heart more closely reflecting the attitudes of the shepherds of Israel. When we take full stock in our calling as shepherds, the work of ministry becomes more than checking things off a to-do list. It involves every fiber of our being. The life of a minister requires sacrificial love. We explore some concrete ways to love and care for the flock later in this lesson.

Yet a shepherd can only fulfill her duties when she is trusted completely by her members. We must first earn the people's trust. That doesn't happen right away. As Wallace Alston, Jr. observes, "The minister must have access to people who are willing to give him a hearing in order to have an effective ministry in any given place."[14] We secure the trust of the flock when we adopt the lifestyle of a loving, faithful shepherd. Get acclimated to the pastor's life by first seeking to become a shepherd who is pleasing to God.

The Pastor as Preacher and Teacher

A significant part of what it means to be a shepherd/elder/pastor involves preaching and teaching the word of God. In the pastoral epistles, for instance, the work and responsibility of teaching is the only competency mentioned by Paul concerning elders (see 1 Tim 3:2; 2 Tim 2:24; and Titus 1:9). Teaching and preaching demand our blood, sweat, and tears. The number of hours it requires to prepare a sermon or teach a Bible study shouldn't be shortchanged.[15] That means if you are a senior pastor, resolve yourself to guard your sermon preparation time. I can't designate precisely how much time we should devote to our preaching and teaching ministries. Thom Rainer once conducted an informal poll with pastors and found that the highest percentage (24 percent) spent thirteen to fifteen hours per week on a sermon.[16] The prescribed hours it takes to marinate and cook every sermon and Bible study will fluctuate. Some preparations take more time while others take less.

14. Alston, Jr., "What a Minister," 254.

15. For instance, Huguley, in *8 Hours or Less*, suggests that due to having many pastoral responsibilities pastors can spend fewer hours on sermons and still be effective. I disagree with this as a general ministry philosophy. We should seek to devote more time and not less time to our sermons and Bible teaching.

16. Rainer, "How Much Time."

During my seminary days, I served as a part-time youth pastor. The youth group held separate services from the adult congregation. Thus I was expected to deliver a word from God every Sunday. Placing my role as a seminary student first, I often let sermon preparation slide. I spent at best ten hours per week on a Sunday message and at worst a few hours. As a side note, if we are serving a church during our seminary training for field units or mentored ministry credits, we should fulfill the contracted hours in a given week. Put in your hours at church and give the congregants your best when you're there and when you're preparing for ministry duties. However, for seminarians, remember that the precious time you set apart for theological training is primary and church ministry is secondary (i.e., during this season). I frequently remind students that they have a lifetime to do ministry but only a few years to learn intensively in a seminary environment. Focus on your studies as much as possible.

As a full-time senior pastor, there is no justification for sloppy or extemporaneous preaching. Yes, on occasion, life crises occur unannounced. Yet as a shepherd, one of our primary tasks is to feed the flock a nutritional, balanced diet, the full counsel of God. Over the last few decades, I have witnessed an ever-growing number of preachers who are not exegeting the Scriptures during their sermons. Their sermons are light in biblical content and exegesis. While a Scripture text may have been read during the worship service, the actual content of the message dances around the text and rarely refers to the Scripture reference in any meaningful way. Most of the thirty or forty minutes is spent telling humorous stories, personal anecdotes, and other illustrations. It saddens me to think that this is the only Bible teaching congregants receive in their week. We can do better.

One of the primary responsibilities of a pastor is to be a preacher and teacher. If you are a solo pastor, most of this instruction rests on you. Not only did I open up God's word every Sunday from the pulpit, but I also led a small group Bible study on Wednesday nights as well as preparing a Bible study or sermon for Friday night gatherings. Several times per year I would also teach a Bible study series on Sunday afternoons open to the entire congregation. The late Haddon Robinson shares, "In the morning, a pastor sets aside time for study. He has to be a scholar. People in the congregation expect a minister to know the Scriptures and to know how to apply them to their daily lives."[17] For this reason, I locked myself in my study, concentrated, and devoted significant hours for preaching and teaching engagements.

17. Robinson, "Preaching Priorities," 154.

Depending on your situation, I encourage you to reserve one third to one half of your weekly hours to purposeful study (fifteen to twenty hours) and stay focused on the task at hand.

Generally speaking, pastors must be ready to preach at any given moment. As Paul writes to Timothy, "Preach the word; be prepared in season and out of season; correct, rebuke and encourage—with great patience and careful instruction" (2 Tim 4:2). Heed his advice. He knows what he's talking about. Commonly, I opened God's word with little or no warning. For example, as a younger congregation, our church welcomed many newborns into the spiritual family. I was expected to share a word from God when I visited the parents of a newborn at the hospital and even when I attended birthday parties. Every so often, I received no notice. "Hey Pastor, would you mind sharing from the word?" Every year, our children's ministry celebrated Fall Festival rather than Halloween. The very first time I was standing around waiting for the festivities to start when one of the leaders invited me to give the children a short message to kick off the event. It happens more often than we'd like. Thankfully, God led me to a few verses explaining to the children why Christians don't rejoice in the Night of the Dead. So be ready to preach and teach at all times.

Another caveat concerning preaching, especially for new pastors, is to be who you are from the pulpit. Through trial and error, find a style of preaching that suits you. It takes rehearsal and repetition to develop your own God-given voice with respect to how you will construct and deliver a sermon. There's no magic number of sermons you must preach to find your unique voice and style. Be patient with this process. As a young pastor, it seems natural to emulate a popular preacher's communication style or mimic a successful church's ministry philosophy. With easy access to online sermons and podcasts, we can be tempted to borrow a sermon from someone we respect—especially when we feel a time crunch.[18] We assume that since a sermon series worked in one setting, those sermons are transferable to every congregation. Remember, your congregation is unique. Your church's areas for developing in discipleship and maturity are unique.[19] You are unique. Be true to your God-given personality and let your preaching flow out of who God has created you to be.

---

18. See Gibson, *Should We Use Someone Else's Sermon?*
19. See Gibson, *Preaching with a Plan*. See also Gallaty and Swain, *Replicate*.

The Pastor as Equipper

Akin to preaching and teaching, David Horner makes the astute observation from Paul's Letter to the Ephesians that pastors are needed "to equip the saints for the work of ministry, for building up the body of Christ" (Eph 4:12). Why equip others for ministry? Contrary to popular belief, we're not supposed to do everything under the sun. Our function is to enable others to participate in God's kingdom work. As Horner explains, "the New Testament teaches that *every member is a minister.*"[20]

If you are privy to a pastoral team, distribute the work based on each person's gifts and interests. Micah Fries and Jeremy Maxfield call this equipping process "leveling the church."[21] They write, "While a leader may get away with riding solo for a while, even earning a legendary mystique as more-than-human, ministry was never intended to be done alone. You can't—and shouldn't—do it all."[22] As you get to know people, their gifts, and their character, be active in distributing the ministry. Especially early on, avoid taking on additional projects and duties outside of your intended job description. Consistently doing so will contribute to burnout and fatigue. If you are a solo pastor, divide responsibilities among your church leadership. To your surprise, many will be pleased to share in the labor. They'll be delighted you trust them enough to ask.

As an equipper, our goal is to educate and model a life of ministry and service. First, we must be perpetual students, lifelong learners. Leanne Van Dyk underscores: "The rapid pace of change in the ministry and the multiple demands on the pastor mean that the M.Div. degree is the entry point, not the finish line, of theological education. A plan for lifelong learning can serve as one tool to encourage, strengthen and deepen the pastor."[23] Through exercising what we read and learn, we instruct our congregants from Scripture what a godly lifestyle invokes.

During my first year as senior pastor, I confess that I set the bar extremely low. For small group meetings, instead of immersing ourselves in God's word, I taught biblical principles via reading popular Christian inspirational books. Precious time was squandered on feel-good stories rather than swallowing the full dosage of God's word. People eventually got fed

---

20. Horner, *Practical Guide for Life and Ministry*, 94–95.
21. Fries and Maxfield, *Leveling the Church*.
22. Fries and Maxfield, *Leveling the Church*, 11.
23. Van Dyk, "Learning the Life," 32.

up, saying, "Matt, why don't we just read the Bible instead of these pointless books?" I learned a lesson quickly. Equip the saints with the word of God. Instruct them on how to be Christlike.

Second, they must see with their own eyes Christian living in action. It's our job as shepherds not only to convey the gospel but also to live it. Equipping does not transpire simply through oral communication. Like it or not, our people presume that as pastors we are moral and godly. One time I was playing basketball with a church member when he looked over at me and said, "Matt, it must be difficult for you. I can live however I want to, but you can't." The comment disturbed me at first, but he was speaking the truth. We equip the sheep when they see biblical values being lived out in us. Interestingly, they even noticed how we used our finances. My wife and I are avid movie watchers. Before entering parish life, we purchased a number of DVDs on clearance. One evening, a congregant stopped by the parsonage. Spotting our movie collection, she asked, "Is that how you spend the church's money?" Fairly or unfairly, we are closely observed by our parishioners. Let's be intentional in equipping the saints through committed ministry praxis. Demonstrating the process of sanctification for our church takes concerted effort and discipline. It will safeguard ministry longevity, but more importantly, we'll seek to honor God in every part of our lives.

The Pastor as Counselor

In my ministry context, I was not often sought out for counseling sessions. But I conducted several premarital counseling meetings with engaged couples. Your church members may frequently solicit your listening ear and seek your advice on any number of topics. It depends on the church and its people. Some pastors dedicate an entire day or two per week to counsel individuals. Other pastors, like me, rarely advised parishioners in this way, at least not in a formal sense. Yet, most likely, someone will knock on your door at some point and seek pastoral counsel. Angie Best-Boss writes, "About half the people who seek professional counseling go to a pastor before they will go anywhere else for assistance."[24]

What is our role as pastoral counselors? How much can we actually help or hurt others? Pastors will serve as adequate counselors when we keep three things in mind.[25] First, we must remember that counseling involves listening

24. Best-Boss, *Surviving Your First Year*, 48.

25. Best-Boss, *Surviving Your First Year*, 49–53.

and not always succumbing to the urge to dispense advice. It's okay to admit that we don't have all the answers. We often can't and don't.

Second, it is critical that we preserve confidentiality at all costs. Best-Boss asserts, "Information that is shared with you cannot be shared with anyone else, even the member's family."[26] If we are married, that means this confidentiality extends to our spouse. Refrain from the urge to tell them anything. If it's confidential information, it must remain confidential.

Third, we must know our limitations as counselors. It's profitable to read texts on Christian counseling, mental illness, and psychology.[27] Even if we can't receive formal psychological training, we can learn from scholars and practitioners in the field. However, many pastors would admit that they are ill-equipped to offer appropriate counseling—especially beyond the first or second visit. In most cases, we will need the humility to refer a parishioner to a trained (hopefully Christian) mental health professional. A congregant once called me to ask if I knew a counselor or psychologist who could guide him through stress management. I hadn't done my homework. It took several weeks for me to procure a name and contact number. Be proactive in searching during your first six months for mental health agencies in your community before the time comes for a referral.

Biblical counseling is a central part of what we do as pastors. Wise counsel flows out of biblical principles that guide our members. The Bible should be the supreme authority that governs how we live. It is our road map for life. We want our parishioners to receive healing for their wounds and direct their paths toward God. Trust him and pray for his wisdom in caring for the flock as a counselor.

The Pastor and Meetings

Without fail, all pastors have meetings to attend and facilitate. As a general rule, the more bodies you have strolling through the halls of your church, the more meetings you'll require. The same holds true for additional pastoral staff. In seminary, the only meetings we had were with friends or with seminary professors. But meetings are part of the ecclesial terrain. We just get used to them. A regular commitment of your week will be centered on meetings.

26. Best-Boss, *Surviving Your First Year*, 50.

27. See Bloem, *Pastoral Handbook of Mental Illness,* and Thomas, ed., *Counseling Techniques.*

Sometimes our meetings are one on one. You may have coffee with a parishioner who is experiencing hardship in his life, and he wants you to pray with him. We may have lunch with a church leader who's having an interpersonal conflict with someone in the congregation. On occasion, we may initiate dialogue with a certain member who's disrupting church life through their divisive behavior. Perhaps an individual has pursued you for a mentoring relationship. Sometimes we visit the hospital to give attention to an ailing congregant.

Our meetings may also involve several people. We meet at church with the elder board or with the deacons. We take the volunteer Sunday school teachers out for an appreciation dinner. We assemble the entire pastoral team to talk shop and pray together. We train and debrief with our small group leaders. Meetings are essential in the life of a church. The important thing is how to manage them and know our limits.

If we're not careful, we can meet with people from sunup to sundown. Meetings can become endless. I was talking with a pastor friend who shared how during his single years he would meet up with multiple people a day, several times a week. Especially in the early stages of ministry, we don't want to disappoint anyone. It's easy to take on more than we can handle. Set some boundaries. Henry Cloud and John Townsend believe many Christians suffer from a life without boundaries. As a result, life becomes chaotic and unmanageable. They write, "Just as homeowners set physical property lines around their land, we need to set mental, physical, emotional, and spiritual boundaries for our lives to help us distinguish what is our responsibility and what isn't."[28] Especially for pastors, there are some meetings where our presence is absolutely vital and others where it would just be nice to have us around. There is a fine line in determining which is which. I have a pastor friend who decided to forego church budget meetings. From his perspective, his presence actually hindered the overall discussion, especially when it came to speaking about his salary and benefits packages. So he concluded that he would no longer attend financial meetings. In the end, the church board valued his trust in them, and it made for a beautiful partnership. After the first year or two, you'll be able to effectively differentiate between meetings that are mandatory and those where your presence is superfluous.

28. Cloud and Townsend, *Boundaries*, 25.

The Pastor as Servant

It's always crucial to be mindful that shepherds are servants in the full sense of the word. In Greek, the word for servant is *diakonos*. It's where we get our word for deacon. The image is comparable to a busboy or someone who waits on tables.[29] If we're honest, most pastors didn't sign up to be waiters/servers who clean up after others. Perhaps we envisioned a cushy job behind a desk where we wouldn't be bothered by people. But that's not the life of a ministry servant. We get our hands dirty, and sometimes we have to pick up the mess around us.

If we believe in professionalism, we won't serve the body of Christ. Today many pastors are well educated. They not only have bachelor's degrees, but a growing number also have several graduate degrees including doctorates. If we equate education with entitlement, pastors will be some of the last people to serve others. Scott M. Gibson observes, "Over the years I have met many diligent, responsible pastors. I have also met lazy pastors who are not only physically lazy, but also intellectually lazy. The two seem to converge and produce a pastor who wants to be pastored rather than being pastor himself."[30]

Many pastors also struggle with pride. We may feel that our credentials permit us to receive service rather than give it. However, Kent and Barbara Hughes remind us that there is success in serving others. They explain, "Everything about Jesus' life shouts service! And the ultimate expression of his servanthood was the cross. There, hanging on the cross, was the Servant *par excellence*, performing the ultimate service."[31]

Ministers are servants in every aspect. There are many facets to service. Sometimes we get on our hands and knees to pick up crumbs left by the children. At other times, we print and fold all the Sunday bulletins. Service takes the form of washing the dishes after a Sunday meal together. It may involve helping an elderly person get into her vehicle. Ministry service might include shivering in the cold, harsh night of winter when assisting someone with a flat tire. It can mean holding a dying person's hand at the hospital as he waits for his heavenly Father to take him home. It may involve weekly visits discipling someone at the local homeless shelter. Opportunities for service are limitless if we choose to follow the master's

29. Mounce, ed., *Mounce's Complete Expository Dictionary*, 63.

30. Gibson, *Should We Use Someone Else's Sermon?*, 58.

31. Hughes and Hughes, *Liberating Ministry from the Success Syndrome*, 50.

example. Get acclimated to the pastor's life by becoming a humble servant. Let's take our ministry cues from Jesus, who said himself, "For even the Son of Man did not come to be served, but to serve, and to give his life as a ransom for many" (Mark 10:45).

The Pastor as Pray-er

Prayer is priceless in the life of a pastor. It is the glue that holds everything together. Prayer is sadly overlooked by pastors, but we need to pray for God to work in and through our lives. In *Working the Angles*, Eugene Peterson writes, "For the majority of the Christian centuries most pastors have been convinced that prayer is the central and essential act for maintaining the essential shape of the ministry to which they were ordained."[32]

Ironically, while pastors are expected to have a vibrant prayer life, many struggle daily to surrender that time to God. I will speak more specifically on the topic of spiritual disciplines in lesson 4. During the week, I would pull out my church directory and pray daily for the congregation. I divided up the list and prayed for certain individuals and families on specific days. While I confess that there were some days when busyness or laziness kicked in, I tried my best to pray regularly and consistently for the church. When I look back on my time there, I always wish that I had prayed more.

To encourage the congregation to pray together, we had a weekly prayer meeting each Saturday morning at church. We studied a Bible chapter together and prayed both corporately and privately afterward. Although this prayer meeting was designated for the leadership of the church and our members, I needed this more prescribed prayer meeting to strengthen my prayer life. On Saturday mornings, I also took intentional time to confess personal and corporate sins. I prayed for my nuclear family as well as for my church family. I prayed for perseverance and joy among the church's leaders. I prayed for the missionaries we supported. I prayed for the Sunday worship service for the Holy Spirit to speak powerfully into our lives and challenge us to be the church that God calls us to be. I prayed for God's wisdom and direction for the church's future steps.

The number of topics we can ask God for are endless. Richard Foster likens prayer to the door of God's heart.[33] To walk through that door, we must choose to pray. Prayer is difficult, I believe, for every person, if they're willing

32. Peterson, *Working the Angles*, 26.
33. Foster, *Prayer*, 2.

to be vulnerable. It's difficult for me. Yet, without prayer, we lack God's love and power. Without prayer, we are empty on the inside and have nothing left to give our parishioners. Without prayer, we lack wisdom and humility. In other words, without prayer, we cease to be pastors.

Acclimate Your Family to Ministry

While our people demand our time and attention, we are also commanded by Scripture to lead and care for our families. As 1 Timothy 3:1–5 instructs,

> Whoever aspires to be an overseer desires a noble task. Now the overseer is to be above reproach, faithful to his wife, temperate, self-controlled, respectable, hospitable, able to teach, not given to drunkenness, not violent but gentle, not quarrelsome, not a lover of money. He must manage his own family well and see that his children obey him, and he must do so in a manner worthy of full respect. (If anyone does not know how to manage his own family, how can he take care of God's church?)

We will benefit from Paul's words of caution.

Make Sure Your Spouse Is on Board

Before we can proceed with our pastoral call, it's critical to have the full support of our spouses (if applicable). Many effective pastors have had their ministry careers terminated prematurely because their spouses were not on the same page. Part of the challenge is the spoken and tacit expectations placed on the spouse of the pastor, typically pastors' wives. Angie Best-Boss writes,

> In the same way, a pastor's spouse needs to be able to enjoy fellowship in the church. Most clergy spouses have felt the frustration of being expected to do a church activity because they are married to the pastor. For many years, the pastor's wife was supposed to play the piano, sing in the choir, teach Sunday school, and participate in, if not lead, the women's ministry.[34]

Lisa Takeuchi Cullen considers some of the tensions of being a pastor's spouse, in this case a pastor's wife. Cullen states, "The basic job description

---

34. Best-Boss, *Surviving Your First Year*, 72.

for pastors' wives hasn't changed in a century. But pastors' wives have."[35] In a rapidly progressive environment such as ours, where pastors' wives pursue their own careers, care for their families, write books, articles, and blogs, air podcasts, and enjoy personal hobbies, the office of the pastor's wife has changed considerably. With such high demands placed on a pastor and the family, Cullen reports sadly that the divorce rate among Christian pastors is no different from the rest of society at 50 percent.[36]

What Cullen's finding suggests is the magnitude of having our spouses fully on board with our ministry calling and communicating in detail what is and isn't expected of them. For instance, part of the strain on relationships is that 84 percent of pastors' wives admit that they have no idea what it means to serve in this capacity.[37] From the outset, we must be clear with the congregation what our spouse will and won't do. The more gifted the spouse is for ministry, the higher the expectation. For example, my wife had extensive ministry experience in teaching children, administration, college ministry, and outreach. Some church leaders may have seen us as a two-for-one opportunity where we would both serve the church and be paid one salary. However, early on, we established that Sarah would only serve others out of her own volition. While she still impacted the church positively on a number of levels, including leading a small group of women and showing hospitality in our home each week, she maintained her boundaries as a pastor's spouse.

Similarly, we have friends serving in pastoral ministry who modeled this marriage and ministry partnership beautifully. Julie was called to pastoral ministry, while Simon worked in the business world. Julie went to seminary for her theological training and later received an esteemed scholarship to study preaching overseas. Simon worked and supported Julie as she pursued her graduate degrees. Later, as Julie eventually became the senior pastor of a church, Simon helped her to fulfill her pastoral duties behind the scenes by caring for their sons and other domestic tasks so that she could serve effectively at church. In short, Simon valued Julie's ministry, and together they formed a mutual partnership to serve God to the fullest.

If you are dating or engaged, be sure your "significant other" or fiancé is absolutely supportive of your calling. Have lengthy discussions with your potential spouse about what his or her concerns are as you enter the pastorate.

35. Cullen, "Pastors' Wives," 47.

36. Cullen, "Pastors' Wives," 47.

37. Cullen, "Pastors' Wives," 48.

To the best of your ability, set specific boundaries together with respect to what your office hours will be, how many evenings you will spend away from home, and how you will maintain a healthy marriage and family life.

Spend Time with Your Family

If you ask pastors what they regret most in their lives, I would imagine that many lament not spending more time with their families. It's the struggle of all pastors to balance time spent with family and fulfilling church responsibilities. At all costs, we must protect family time. Roger Ball says, "New opportunities excite me and can get me in trouble. I've learned to say no. Guarding personal family time is a must."[38]

The tendency for clergy is to dump domestic responsibilities on our spouses. For some reason, we believe that our calling as pastors is more significant than our spouse's responsibilities at work or in the home. By doing so, we simply leave our loved ones behind to take care of everything. Others conform to the ministry axiom, "If I take care of God's business, God will take care of my family."[39] This negligent thinking will wreck our ministries and our families. God commands pastors to faithfully display love and support to our spouse and children. As Paul instructs Timothy, if we can't lead our family, we can't expect to lead the bride of Christ.

In his book *The Pastor's Family*, Daniel Langford responds to the epidemic plaguing America's pastors in their disregard for the family unit. Langford conveys the biting repercussions of pastors who continuously overlook the requests of their spouses and kids. He states, "The pursuit of a pastor toward his calling to the exclusion of his children and their needs has created an almost ubiquitous resentment of preachers' children toward their fathers. When they become adults, many grieve the loss of the time they never had with their pastor dads."[40] The primary channel to reverse this damaging trend in the pastorate is to place higher value on what our families think of us than on what our parishioners do. We can improve the way our families view our vocation as pastors by our example. When we choose to put them first, we testify that our involvement in ministry life can be a blessing and not a curse.

---

38. Ball, "Initiating Dialogue," 127.

39. Shelley, *Healthy Hectic Home*, 65.

40. Langford, *Pastor's Family*, 11.

Marshall Shelley shares an anecdote of a pastor who promised his son that they would spend quality time together. They were prepared to embark on the afternoon's excursion when an elder of the church interrupted the outing. He shared how a couple in the church was offended, on the verge of leaving the church, and that the pastor needed to attend to them immediately. As his son watched this verbal exchange, the pastor politely responded that he was going hunting with his son now and would deal with that situation later. He recounts the following:

> Wilbur's face got red. "If you go hunting, don't bother coming back." Then he turned to get back into his car. "I don't think you mean that, Wilbur," the pastor said, "I'll see you in church tomorrow." The pastor's son reflects, "As Dad and I headed off to the woods, I had to ask, 'Is this going to cost you your job?' 'I don't think so,' Dad said. 'But if it does, the job is not worth keeping.'"[41]

We are making a conscious decision when we continue to put the needs of the church ahead of our family. Let's invest our time, energy, and resources on our families first.[42] As one Gordon-Conwell student expressed accurately, "Your family is your first ministry." Spend time with your spouse. Spend time with your children. It's not easy to be a pastor's kid, also known as a "PK," as Barnabas Piper admits, "The life of a PK is complex, occasionally messy, often frustrating, and sometimes downright maddening."[43] Congregations may come and go, but if we do what's right, our families will join us for the rest of the ministry ride.

Unless you dive right in, you can't fully comprehend what the pastorate will require of you. In this lesson, we've offered a glimpse into what it's like being a pastor. I've presented some of the major responsibilities and challenges of being in parish ministry. But at the end of the day, your experience will be unique to you. It can't be duplicated. However, my hope is that I have touched on topics that all ministers come across in the early parts of their careers. In the following lesson, we talk about creating healthy habits that will hopefully catalyze a jovial and holistic lifestyle in the pastorate.

---

41. Shelley, *Healthy Hectic Home*, 101–2.
42. See Batten, *Parenting by Faith*.
43. Piper, *Pastor's Kid*, 16.

Ask Yourself

1. As I begin pastoral ministry, what will I focus on first, second, and third?

2. What do I see as my unique roles as a pastor?

3. What are the expectations that I have for the church, and what will they expect from me?

4. How will I guard time spent with my family?

4

Create Healthy Habits

The Exodus of Ministers

THEY SAY THAT HABITS develop when a person commits to the same behavior for a few weeks. In life, we pick up all types of habits, both intentionally and unintentionally. Some habits are good for us, like flossing our
teeth or writing thank-you cards. Other habits prove detrimental or even
fatal, like smoking or failing to use our turn signal when changing lanes.
Pastors form various habits during their tenure in ministry. Some habits are
constructive, while others cripple. This lesson emphasizes the importance
of creating healthy habits, especially as we begin our pastoral calling, and
offers some practical suggestions on how to do this.

Pastoral ministry can be taxing even on naturally gifted and extroverted ministerial leaders. As a result, promising members of the clergy are
encountering all kinds of excuses to bail out of the pastorate. Derek Tidball
observes, "In spite of the many who genuinely find ministry satisfying, the
truth has to be faced that many do not."[1] Similarly, Gary Kinnaman and
Alfred Ells write, "Leaders don't seem to be lasting."[2] While ministers are
exiting the pastorate for diverse reasons, I would argue that one of the leading catalysts behind their early departures is a lack of balanced lives. As
pastors, we are solely responsible for our well-being. My encouragement
is for seminarians and new pastors to start their ministries on the right
footing. We don't want to learn this lesson only after we have involuntarily

1. Tidball, *Skillful Shepherds*, 315.
2. Kinnaman and Ells, *Leaders That Last*, 10.

joined the clergy exodus. Create healthy habits early on that will better enable you to serve God for a lifetime.

Clergy Burnout

Burnout rates and health issues continue to soar among pastors. Roy Oswald reports, "Approximately twenty percent of clergy with whom I've worked in seminars score extremely high on the Clergy Burnout Inventory. Among clergy in long pastorates (ten years or more) the number jumps to fifty percent."[3] Rae Jean Proeschold-Bell and Jason Byassee share a disturbing report that "showed clergy submitting more health care claims than the general population."[4] What is burnout, and what are its symptoms? Christina Maslach and Susan Jackson define burnout as "a syndrome of emotional exhaustion and cynicism that occurs frequently among individuals who do 'people-work' of some kind. A key aspect of the burnout syndrome is increased feelings of emotional exhaustion."[5]

Signs of burnout are masked by different guises. Anne Jackson makes this confession:

> Because I loved my job so much, I (proudly) didn't take a single vacation day during my first year on staff. By the end of our summer camp (which I was responsible to manage), I was exhausted. Needless to say, the quickness of the onset of my weariness caught me off guard. The job I had once looked forward to tackling every single workday (and sometimes on my days off) I was now dreading.[6]

In the end, Jackson was forced to take time off from ministry due to her declining emotional and physical condition.

At the end of his first year in pastoral ministry, the late Kenneth Swetland experienced a stroke on one side of his body, attributable to fatigue and burnout. In a moving sermon preached at Gordon-Conwell Theological Seminary's chapel service, Swetland poured out his heart to students about the reality and severity of this destructive emotional, physical, and spiritual condition.

3. Oswald, *Clergy Self-Care*, 3.
4. Proeschold-Bell and Byassee, *Faithful and Fractured*, xvi.
5. Maslach and Jackson, "Measurement," 99.
6. Jackson, *Mad Church Disease*, 32.

In June of 1965, Swetland had just completed his first year as a pastor. After a difficult first year and not much physical exercise, he humorously confessed, "I decided to get in shape all in one day." He rode his bicycle through two neighboring towns and later went home for lunch. As he began to speak to his wife, his words were unrecognizable. He remarked wittily, "The thought of *glossolalia* [speaking in tongues] passed through my mind, but it was not that." His wife called the hospital. By the time the ambulance arrived, his vision blurred, and he was paralyzed on one side. Swetland was then hospitalized for two weeks.

The hospital's chief neurologist named his condition a stress-induced stroke triggered by the bicycle ride, but the true source of the illness originated long before. In that first year of ministry, Swetland admits that he "nearly worked himself to an early grave," not caring for his health. The doctor replied, "There is a God and you are not he. God is God and you are not." If he would rest and take his daily medication, his body would repair itself in time. With that guidance, Swetland began the slow path to recovery. It took an entire year before he could speak full sentences again.[7]

Burnout, in its varied forms, is a serious condition. But it can be avoided if we take the right precautions. As we have seen, it's quite easy to exhaust ourselves during the first years. The recipe for clergy burnout is very clear-cut. Young pastors are overzealous, overworked, and overly eager to please the masses. We forget to take time for vacation, days off, and reflection. We disregard our body's plea for rest. We push our way through fatigue. All too quickly, our congregation takes our foregoing of respite as the norm. If we begin our ministries with minimal time for ourselves and our families, the congregation will expect us to continue down the same path each year. Burnout is just waiting around the corner. In order to prevent burnout in our ministry careers, we must be proactive in seeking wholeness in our lives.

Our Need for Wholeness

God has created us to be whole persons. Just as an integer is a whole number, our bodies don't have separate parts or divisions. They are completely intact. God designed us to be integers by experiencing a healthy balance in all areas of our lives. A natural tendency in every human being is to accentuate our fortes or what we enjoy most, neglecting other vital elements. If we take

7. Swetland, "God is God."

pleasure in learning and studying, we often omit physical exercise from our regimens. If we are carnivores by nature, we don't see the vegetables on our plates or even avoid putting them there in the first place. You get the point.

Becoming a whole individual takes discipline and is a conscious choice. It doesn't happen naturally. We must choose to make it happen. Contrary to some pastors' beliefs, taking care of ourselves is not selfish.[8] Now this calling for personal wholeness is not confined to intellectual pursuits in the form of becoming what the Greeks referred to as a polymath or "a person of great or varied learning."[9] Rather, we are speaking more broadly of becoming well-rounded individuals. We aspire to become people who take in all the diversity that life has to offer: pursuing knowledge, reading fiction and nonfiction, appreciating music and the fine arts, participating in sports and physical activities, engaging in meaningful conversations, and caring for the world and its needs, among other salient tasks. Through this expansive engagement with life, we will find deeper satisfaction and simply make for better ministers.

Pastors model wholeness or the lack thereof to our congregants. As Pete Scazzero observes, "Unless we know what it is to care for ourselves, we can't love others well."[10] Therefore, pastors should not only work diligently but also seek a balanced approach to life. For pastors, the quest for wholeness is not optional. But sadly, the bulk of pastors can't seem to find time for personal well-being. Scazzero continues,

> Most of us are overscheduled and preoccupied; we are starved for time, exhausted from the endless needs around us. Who has time to enjoy Jesus, our spouses, our children, life itself? We assume we'll catch up on our sleep some other time. The space we need for replenishing our soul and relaxing can happen later. Few of us have time for fun and hobbies. We don't have a life! There is simply too much work to be done for God.[11]

Yet balance is the life source that fosters personal and relational effectiveness. The rest of this lesson will offer suggestions on how pastors can create healthy habits and promote balance. We will address four crucial habits of life: emotional habits, physical habits, relational habits, and spiritual habits.

---

8. Proeschold-Bell and Byassee, *Faithful and Fractured*, xviii.

9. *American Heritage Dictionary*, 962.

10. Scazzero, "Skimming."

11. Scazzero, "Skimming."

Emotional Habits

The emotional and psychological demands of ministry require pastors to have solid mental health. As Scott M. Gibson conveys, "Pastors contend with matters that the average person could never imagine: spiritual conflict, relational disappointments, discipleship setbacks, family crises, and personality tensions, among others."[12] By emotional habits, I am referring to matters related to our mental and psychological being. As humans, we experience myriad emotions. We can be happy, sad, excited, depressed, fearful, bored, hopeful, or shameful, among many other feelings, all in one afternoon. The question is whether we have these emotions under our control or whether they control us.

Since our vocation calls for extensive human interaction and the ability to gauge others' emotions, we need a firm handle on our emotional condition. Doctors and mental health counselors are commonly instructed to grow callous to human suffering. "It's not healthy to be on an emotional roller coaster every single day with your patients and clients," they are told. This advice isn't necessarily the best way to deal with emotional stress in the ministry. As pastors, it's nearly impossible to check our emotions at the door when listening to the aches and pains of those we love. And pushing our pejorative emotions under the rug won't help either. There must be a better way to cope.

King David was a man of many emotions. When we read the Psalms, we see a man who desperately tried to rein in his emotions. On scrolls of parchment, David poured out his heart and soul to God. Louise Morganti Kaelin underscores, "The secret to living our best life is to give ourself permission to feel everything, but to not get stuck in the negative emotions."[13] What Kaelin is saying is that we should allow ourselves to feel every kind of emotion. Kaelin continues:

> The emotion is not bigger than we are. Sometimes we are fearful of allowing ourselves to really go with an emotion because it threatens to overwhelm us. In reality, that almost never happens. What makes the feeling so powerful is the energy we put into not admitting we are feeling it. Fear, anger, guilt, and resentment— these are all like small children pulling at your leg. They get louder and louder until you finally ask what they want; 99% of the time,

12. Gibson, *Should We Use Someone Else's Sermon?*, 59–60.

13. Kaelin, "Legalize Your Emotions."

their response is "nothing." What they wanted was your attention, and now that they have it, they can move on.[14]

The danger, according to Kaelin, is in denying that these emotions exist. She believes it's healthier to admit our struggles and pray that we can conquer them with God's help.

One way to monitor our emotions is to write them down in a journal. Some of you may be saying to yourself, "No, thank you." For my seminary graduation, my wife handed me a brand new leather-bound journal. Maybe it's my pride or ego talking, but journaling has never been my thing, either. I was grateful for the gesture, but I never really thought to actually use it. But writing in my journal, on occasion, has become healing water for my soul, especially during rough seasons in my life. In this journal, I not only share my hardships with God but also write down moments where he has been faithful, merciful, and kind.

In the Psalms, we get a peek into the true persona of David, a human being who left no emotion unspoken. By writing down his emotions and reading them, David repaired his soul and recognized many of his emotional hang-ups. These psalms served as prayers of confession, triumph, despair, and pleas for help. Give yourself the opportunity to feel every emotion, and give them to God for restoration and healing.

Second, laughter is a necessary emotional habit that I would endorse in the life of any minister. There's a reason people love to watch comedies and television shows or spend an evening listening to a stand-up comic. People like to be amused and enjoy a good laugh. We need to learn how to laugh at ourselves, our failures, and our life circumstances and not take ourselves and everything so seriously.

As the firstborn son and the eldest of three boys in an Asian American family, laughing didn't come naturally for me. With the weight of my immigrant parents' expectations on my shoulders, I was overly serious about life, school, family responsibilities, church, competitive sports, and everything. This inability to lighten up and laugh at myself sprung from my inherent affinity toward success. Though it went unspoken, I was always expected by my parents to perform at a high level. I felt like I couldn't slack off morally, spiritually, educationally, or in anything. The voice in my head never left me: "What kind of role model would you be for your younger brothers if you failed?"

14. Kaelin, "Legalize Your Emotions."

I've learned over the years to laugh at myself and to lighten up. And I actually do have a sense of humor. Laughing is the best remedy to offset negative emotions in the pastorate. I could always do *something* better, more efficiently, and more effectively. But I trusted that God would still use me as a pastor. It helps that God gave me a wife who is impish. We've learned to laugh with each other and at each other. Laughter takes the edge off of life, and it will enable you to enjoy ministry more.

Our emotions are God-given. We experience them for a reason. However, we can learn to control our emotions and laugh in dire moments. By balancing our emotions we not only become comfortable in our own skin but also draw closer to our creator as we experience all kinds of emotions he designed us to feel.

Physical Habits

Many passages in Scripture refer to the body. For some people, the good news is that we're promised a new one when we enter the gates of heaven. However, in the meantime, God expects us to take care of the one we've been given. In 1 Corinthians 3:16–17, Paul asks, "Don't you know that you yourselves are God's temple and that God's Spirit dwells in your midst? If anyone destroys God's temple, God will destroy that person; for God's temple is sacred, and you together are that temple." As we can see plainly, God cares deeply about his people and so should we care for ourselves.

Diet: What's on Our Plate?

A prerequisite of overseas missionaries is to be able to eat everything placed in front of them. We've all heard stories of missionaries eating insects and animals that we might consume only if paid large sums of money as a contestant on a reality TV show. As pastors, we're similarly expected to eat whatever is served at someone's home. That's where the problem begins. At times, what's on our plates is not the healthiest option, but we don't have a better alternative. It's not easy to tell your host, "Sorry, I don't like what you're serving me." Or, worse, "That's not healthy!" What's on our plate may be fried chicken, French fries, burgers, sausages, sugar-filled sodas, potato chips, tiramisu, and cheesecake.

However, on many occasions, we do have a choice. When we're at a restaurant, for instance, we can make a conscious decision to select healthier entrees and to skip dessert. A larger question is whether we will exhibit self-control. Our diet is such an overlooked facet of pastoral life. But the way we eat can positively or negatively impact our energy level, mood, self-image, and overall health.

Being a Christian for over thirty years, I have met my share of pastors. Like shoes and clothing, pastors come in all shapes and sizes. Since church ministry often involves meeting with people and sharing a meal together, we find ourselves eating frequently, and sometimes we fall prey to gluttony and poor diets. There were times that I shared in one single day three meals (breakfast, lunch, and dinner) with a different parishioner each time. My weekly routine included eating lunch with two or three different church members. Now that can become a lot of eating out and a lot of fast food joints. I shamefully can't tell you how much pizza and Chinese food I consumed during those years.

What we choose to feed our bodies is important. First, it's significant to take good care of the bodies God has given us. We only get one life. Eat a balanced diet. Do you remember what you learned in elementary school? Our teachers reminded us to eat from the four basic food groups: dairy, protein, fruits and vegetables, and carbohydrates. A balanced diet gives us the energy we require to do kingdom work. Be careful of what you consume each day.

Second, at all times, we are setting an example for our congregants and our families. One of the fruit of the Spirit is self-control. We know that self-control involves learning the art of self-care. It's not difficult to become overweight especially in pastoral ministry. Hundreds if not thousands of extra calories can be consumed in an instant. Let's show our church members that we can exercise good judgment even in the little things like our diet. Let's model self-control and take proper care of our bodies.

Exercise: How Often Do We Sweat?

In addition to healthy eating, our bodies appreciate regular physical exercise. As pastors or professors, we are often forced into a sedentary lifestyle. Besides the few minutes we are standing to deliver a sermon, pastors are often sitting down in our studies. Since we have flexibility to determine our hourly schedules, try to fit physical exercise into the weekly calendar. Simply getting a gym membership does not ensure that we'll work out consistently or at all. In their book *Simple Health*, David Biebel and Harold Koenig share an all-too-common example:

> Perhaps you heard about the guy who joined a health club. A year later, he stopped by to renew his $500 membership, but he was even more flabby and out-of-shape. When he mentioned this to the receptionist, she reviewed the record, and said, "Perhaps it would help if you would stop in once in a while."[15]

Before we had children, I was a regular at our local fitness center. I stopped in two to three times per week for one and a half hours each session doing free weights, Nautilus exercises, and cardio. After having children, I confess that I have frequented the gym with diminished regularity. Exercise is hard to come by unless we make it a priority.

Exercise can be an extension of your ministry. For example, as a lover of basketball, when I was a pastor, I spent time with my congregants who shared my passion. For several months in the year, our church participated in a local church-wide basketball league that convened on Sunday evenings. I also coordinated with guys who shared the same day off and played hoops early in the morning. Sometimes exercise came in the form of a morning jog or going out with my sons for a walk during the lunch hour. I know pastors who play tennis or racquetball with church members. Be innovative and create pockets of time to exercise. However, don't take your freedom for granted. I heard of a pastor who loved golf and played several rounds per week whether on his own or in the company of a select few church members. Eventually, he was asked to resign for what some deemed an abuse of the church's work hours.

The statistics never cease on how exercise benefits the overall quality of our lives. Biebel and Koenig state, "Regular physical activity reduces your risk of coronary heart disease, stroke, and colon cancer. Regular physical activity reduces the risk of developing type 2 diabetes or high blood pressure. . . . Regular physical activity can help reduce stress and feelings of depression and anxiety. Regular physical activity can help relieve or prevent back pain."[16] The list goes on and on.

When I was a pastor, I used to feel guilty when I went to the gym. I thought there were more productive ways to use my time. One day, however, I was asked by one of our ministry leaders who happened to be a physician,

---

15. Biebel and Koenig, *Simple Health*, 47.
16. Biebel and Koenig, *Simple Health*, 47.

"Are you getting regular exercise?" At the time, I wasn't and I said so. He responded, "Make sure you frequent the gym. We want you to be a happy pastor." So don't feel remorseful about going to the gym. Carve out time for regular exercise. You'll be glad you did and so will your parishioners.

Relaxation: When Do I Find Time to Rest?

Being a pastor is never a nine-to-five job. It's a calling that has no set hours. That can be difficult for us and for our family. When our church members need us, we should be present. That being the case, many pastors are stretched for time. In caring for the individuals and families in our churches, when is there actually time for personal rest and relaxation?

One of the greatest things about being a pastor is that, in general, we control our schedules. Yes, there is some rigidity in a pastor's week. Meetings are scheduled for certain mornings or evenings. We may not be able to alter the time of our weekly pastoral staff meetings, elder/deacon meetings, small groups, Bible studies, or prayer meetings. The emergencies of life demand our attention, such as an accident, a personal crisis, or death. But on the whole, we are the arbiters of how we spend our time. For some, that's a negative element, because we aren't adept at time management. For others, it's a pastoral perk that we enjoy.

God knows that we need rest. That's why he created the Sabbath. He didn't rest because he was tired but to set an example for us. He knew that for some of us our penchant for success or being well liked would drive us to become workaholics. Somehow we convince ourselves that staying busy is the way we should live. Yet the Bible makes it clear that one day a week should be reserved for respite.

What can you do on your Sabbath? Plenty! Spend some extended quiet time with the Father. Go out and explore the beauty of your state. Play with your children at the park. Go for a swim or go for a walk with your spouse. Take an afternoon nap. Read that long-awaited book while you enjoy a cup of coffee. Exercise. Get your mind off work and allow your body to take pleasure in a favorite hobby.

Our bodies tell us when we're not resting enough. We're cranky and brusque with others. We dislike what we're doing. We find ourselves dreaming about a seven-day cruise in the Caribbean. We're more vulnerable to temptation and sin. We feel discouraged or depressed during our waking moments. So do yourself a favor and care for your physical health.

Relational Habits

There are varying philosophies regarding pastors and friendships. One perspective is to actively pursue intimate friendships with members of your church family. On the other hand, I've also been warned that pastors should not seek out close friends with parishioners. End of story. If a pastor cannot pursue an intimate friendship within the confines of the church, where is she to turn for support? Everyone, including pastors, needs a friend and a confidant![17]

For married pastors, hope for friendship lies naturally in our spouse. In a healthy marriage, our spouse is the person with whom we confide in all matters. Of course, he or she is the primary person we look to for acceptance, wisdom, and friendship. But not all spouses are supportive of our ministerial call, nor can we expect to disclose every hardship with him. Where can we find additional sounding boards and encouragers?

Make a Friend in the Ministry

Pastors are some of the loneliest people I know. As Gary Kinnaman testifies, "Most people in full-time ministry do not have close personal friendships and consequently are alarmingly lonely and dangerously vulnerable."[18] For this reason, it seems natural that relationships could be explored through befriending other pastors. Kenneth Swetland maintains, "This speaks of the need for pastors to cultivate friendships with other pastors who can offer knowledgeable support and counsel in a way no one else can. Such people can provide both affirmation and helpful criticism when needed. Too many pastors settle for cordiality with other ministers when collegiality is what is needed."[19]

Building a friendship with a pastor in your city can be cumbersome. Several factors impede the pathway to friendship between fellow clergy. Sometimes we can't agree on particular doctrines or philosophies of ministry. These theological distinctions become our convenient way out of a potential friendship, because many of us prefer to be alone.

What is more, pastors battle all types of insecurities when they compare themselves with others. I remember during my first year in Denver a

17. See Horn, *Soulmates,* and Robert, *Faithful Friendships.*
18. Kinnaman and Ells, *Leaders That Last,* 10.
19. Swetland, *Hidden World of the Pastor,* 14.

local pastor invited some ministers in the area for dinner. The air felt stuffy and awkward. Questions were flung freely concerning numbers like, "How many couples do you have in your church?" or "What's the annual budget?" It seemed like the evening's agenda was to size up the competition in the room and ascertain whether we measured up.

Dean Shriver describes a common struggle with pastoral insecurity that he admits concerning his neighboring church planter. He writes,

> We had started our ministries at the same time. But we sure didn't seem to be reaping the same fruit or enjoying the same benefits. "Lord," I demanded, "why is his house nicer and his view more picturesque than mine? Why's he got a three-car garage when I have no garage at all? Why has his church grown more? Why is he more 'successful' than me?" These were ugly questions— wicked insecurities exposing a heart infected by coveting and sinful discontent.[20]

What we must come to embrace, especially as pastors, is that God blesses each person differently. We must overcome pettiness and cease the territorialism that hampers our effectiveness. Individual churches are not conglomerates. We work for the same employer whose name is God.

Like a rare gem, there are certain pastors with whom we can dialogue beyond the numbers. It may take our initiative, but it's well worth the effort. For instance, I met up with a pastor who is several years older than me and had been established for nearly two decades in the Colorado area. I decided to contact him and have lunch together. We met at a local restaurant, and during that hour not once did we bring up church membership or finances. Instead, we simply shared our joys and struggles about our respective ministries. Our time together was refreshing.

I often tell my students that one of their number of homework assignments in seminary is to find a "best friend" in ministry. Pray and ask God to bless you with at least one close friend. A person you can be friends with for a lifetime. A person who gives as well as receives. A person who accepts you for who you are. A person who will not judge you when you vent your frustrations or anger. A person who genuinely loves you and cares for you. A person who can speak truth into your life and even correct and rebuke you. A person who will not desert you, gossip about you, or turn his or her back on you. Friendships among pastors are possible, but we need to mitigate our insecurities and place value in things that truly matter.

20. Shriver, *Nobody's Perfect*, 60.

Find a Spiritual Mentor

Not only should we focus early on to find ministry partners and friends, but young pastors also will benefit significantly from having pastoral mentors and spiritual advisors. Carrie Doehring recounts,

> My first year, when I encountered many aspects of ministry for the first time, was like a supervisor-less internship year. . . . The challenges of constructing the public persona of being a minister was made more difficult by the fact that I had no office outside the study in my home, and no staff to whom I related on a daily basis. I often sought advice from the only other ordained woman in my presbytery, a second-career clergywoman, who became a mentor.[21]

Spiritual mentors are available, but usually we must seek them out. After my first year in seminary, I felt the glaring absence of a spiritual mentor. My parents had been praying all year that I would find a mentor who would take me under his wings and model the pastoral life for a young seminarian. During the first year, I noticed one particular faculty member who was disarmingly friendly and personable. He happened to teach courses in the areas of preaching and ministry. He's kindly written the foreword to this book.

One day I stirred up the courage to send him my testimony and even my resume. Since I never had a mentor, that's how I thought these things worked. I then asked if he would consider meeting with me. Several days later, we met over the lunch hour, and he stressed the importance of prayer in seeking how the Lord may lead this possible relationship. A week later he became my mentor, making a commitment to me not only for the rest of my seminary years but gratefully for life.

My mentor and I are not limited only to conversations about being a pastor. He keeps me accountable in every facet of life. Even in the most vulnerable topics like sexual purity, he has held me to account so that I can strive for godly obedience. The reason I can be candid in this relationship is because I am confident in his pastoral love for me. I can't express in words how grateful I am to have a person like him in my life. Every person needs a spiritual mentor, in particular, pastoral leaders. Seminarians, if you haven't done so already, pray and search for a spiritual mentor. He or she may be a professor at your seminary or a trusted pastor.

21. Doehring, "Fragile Connections," 92.

Get Some Accountability, Please!

Accountability is critical in pastoral ministry. It is a must. We need people in our lives that will ask us tough questions and do everything humanly possible to prevent us from sinning or from making a monumental mistake. Proverbs 18:24 helpfully points out that "One who has unreliable friends soon comes to ruin, but there is a friend who sticks closer than a brother." That kind of friendship is rare, but it is possible. To surmount the temptations of life and ministry, we need such a friend and accountability partner.

As mentioned, a great place to find such a colleague in life is seminary. At no other time in one's life (other than perhaps during college) will you find similar people who share your passions to love God and love people. I was blessed to find my accountability partner and best friend during my first year of seminary. Steve lived at the end of the dormitory hallway. At the time I wasn't intentional about finding such a close friend, but Steve was God's gracious gift to me.

On paper, Steve and I had very little in common except for our love of basketball. In fact, in one of my first encounters with him, I unintentionally offended him with a comment that I had made which he later told me about. Faux pas in speech will happen. Friendship introduces mistake-making. But over the years we've learned to accept one another's idiosyncrasies and have had the freedom to discuss difficult issues. Even though we've encountered our share of misunderstandings, we trust each other and love each other like David loved Jonathan. We can bare our souls to one another and share our darkest sins. We challenge each other to live a holy life. This kind of friendship develops with much time and sacrifice, but it's critical to our lives. Find an accountability partner as soon as you can.

Spiritual Habits

One of my biggest regrets in seminary was the inability to monitor my spiritual health. Exercising spiritual disciplines has never been my forte. Reading the Bible, praying, and fasting have always been more difficult for me than a delight. Perhaps you can resonate with such feelings. During seminary, the excuse I relied on most heavily was a seminarian's famous last words: "When I become a full-time pastor, I'll focus on my spiritual life. I don't have time now, but I'll have time later on." As a full-time pastor, the situation didn't improved all that much. There was even less time to devote to spiritual devotions. In actuality, it was never a matter of time. It was a matter of the heart. It still is. We must be vigilant in spending time with God. It means everything for the Christian and everything for the pastor.

Spiritual dryness is not unique among pastors. Angie Best-Boss says, "Cultivation of personal spiritual growth is perhaps one of the most neglected areas of pastors' lives. We spend so much time caring for others' spiritual needs and concerns that our own spirituality gets left on the back burner."[22] One study showed that "62 percent of ministers have little spiritual life! Excessive demands on time, conflicts within congregations and between ministers and members, loss of personal spiritual life and loneliness account for a deep malaise within our professional and personal lives."[23] But are we compromising ourselves and our people with a negligent spiritual life?

Jesus is our model for spiritual upkeeping. The God incarnate waged war within his soul to maintain a consistent and open relationship with the Father. Spending isolated moments with God was his lifeline. Throughout the gospels, we see a plethora of examples where Jesus left the company of his disciples and the crowds to share what was on his heart with his Father. How much more do we as finite beings require God's vital connection in our lives? Ken Blanchard and Phil Hodges encourage,

> Your habits are how you renew your daily commitment as a leader to serve rather than to be served. As a leader committed to serve despite all the pressures, trials, and temptations He faced, how did Jesus replenish His energy and servant perspective? His habits! Through a life pattern of solitude and prayer, knowledge of the will of God expressed in His Holy Word, and the community He shared with a small group of intimate companions, Jesus was constantly refreshed and renewed.[24]

The inability to recharge spiritually on a consistent basis is, I believe, one of the leading catalysts in a pastor's discontentment with ministry. I have felt this growing chasm within my soul. It stole my happiness and corroded my joy. Bruce Demarest reminds, "Many of us know our Bibles, and our theology is sound. But when we're honest, joy, peace, and power seem to be missing. We hunger for a sense of God's presence and long for a connectedness

---

22. Best-Boss, *Surviving Your First Year*, 77.

23. Purves, *Crucifixion of Ministry*, 17.

24. Blanchard and Hodges, *Lead Like Jesus*, 33.

with Him that will make us come alive at the core of our being."[25] In other words, we go through the motions of pastoral ministry with our heart and soul utterly disengaged from the whole experience.

There is a direct correlation between our spiritual health and how satisfied we are in life. For example, William Hulme and his colleagues observe: "By contrast, those clergy feeling satisfied with their prayer and devotional life tend also to feel satisfied with their marital and family life, their ministry, with the support from the congregation, and with the respect shown them by congregational and denominational leaders."[26] Similarly, when I'm less in tune with God, the more I want God to give me a free pass out of parish life. When I'm not aligned with Jesus in daily communication, I become less gracious toward others and more accusatory. When I don't care for my spiritual health, I am more easily discouraged and decreasingly optimistic about what God can accomplish. And all these negative symptoms arise out of a lack of meaningful time rendered to the Lord.

As pastors, there is little excuse for a nonexistent spiritual life. It's critical that we make time for developing our relationship with God, especially since we call our parishioners to do likewise. If you're a morning person, do your devotions when your children are sleeping. If you function best in the afternoon or late at night, allot moments for prayer, quiet reflection, and Scripture reading. It doesn't matter what time of day. In addition, as a pastor, I made it a pattern to listen to others' sermons for personal enrichment. This was not a waste of time. I found that other pastors spoke challenging words of truth into my soul that I needed to hear and put into practice. Do not neglect your soul for the sake of busyness and doing ministry. Eventually our habits of spiritual negligence catch up to us, and we'll lead the church with empty spiritual tanks. The metaphorical car will inevitably crash on the shoulder or topple off a treacherous terrain.

The Juggling Act

Finding balance as a minister can be challenging. I've never been good at juggling. I have tried juggling before with three tennis balls, but I routinely drop one or two. How do we find time to care for our emotional, relational, physical, and spiritual health? We're probably exhausted just thinking about

25. Demarest, *Satisfy Your Soul*, 49.
26. Hulme et al., *Pastors in Ministry*, 45.

the process, but it can be accomplished with discipline. We must guard our time and be diligent when that time is in front of us.

Avoid the temptation to use your family as an excuse for not living a balanced lifestyle. Family time isn't what deters us from a balanced life. We can get in our own way. Haddon Robinson shared a story of how his wife was able to put a positive spin on his rigorous schedule to their young children. Rather than speaking harshly about Daddy's precious time away from home, she asked the kids, "Isn't it great that we get to share daddy with other people?"[27] What a winsome way to communicate the essence of ministry to our children so that they might not become embittered as pastor's children. Yet this question works best when we're active in the lives of our family members when we're home.

We are in control of how we spend our time and what we choose to do with it. We're not always in elder meetings or always working on our sermons or Bible studies. We're not always visiting the sick. We can structure our lives so that we experience wholeness and balance. And to be the most productive person we can for God, our families, our churches, and ourselves, we must carve out time for creating healthy habits. Don't blame the church for sucking life out of you. Make time for yourself and your family. It will help increase your longevity in the pastorate and enable you to lead others more effectively.

Ask Yourself

1. In which areas of my life do I need greater balance?

2. How will I develop healthier habits in those areas of weakness?

3. Do I have a spiritual mentor, close friend, or accountability partner to share my joys and struggles with? If not, how will I find such a person?

4. What will I stop doing to waste time so that I can create balance in my life?

27. Scott M. Gibson, telephone conversation with author, June 4, 2009.

5

Develop Your Leadership Skills

The Introverted Leader

I WAS BORN IN Chicago and raised mostly in suburban Park Ridge. During the seventies and eighties, there was very little racial and ethnic diversity in our town. My brothers and I were frequently on the receiving end of prejudice.[1] Treated differently for my physical appearance, I grew up self-conscious and withdrawn. It didn't help that I was scrawny and needed glasses way too early. I didn't like making eye contact and was quite happy being left alone.

As I entered high school, I still found myself introverted and drained emotionally by lengthy periods of social interaction. But somehow I developed the courage to run for class president during junior year. I pursued student leadership out of aspirations of being accepted at a top college. Later in senior year, I found myself nervously standing to speak in the auditorium in front of a sea of students, their families and friends, school administrators, teachers, and staff. To my amazement, I had been selected by my peers to deliver the leadership speech at the National Honor Society induction ceremony.

For most of my life, I wouldn't have classified myself as the leader type. We often think of leaders as those who are in the limelight or members of the popular crowd. They tend to have big personalities. They tend to emit the fragrance of courage, not the aura of timidity. They tend to enjoy being

1. Tragically, my younger brother, Timothy David Kim, was brutally murdered in Manila, Philippines, on November 7, 2015. See my book *Preaching to People in Pain* for details about Tim.

73

in front of people. They tend to like to be noticed. They tend to like being the center of attention. They tend to like publicly vocalizing ideas.

In *Pastor Paul*, Scot McKnight says it this way: "To pastor people is to be a leader, which for many means extroversion and (as commonly used) *charisma*, which really means 'dynamic personality type.'"[2] None of these traits matched my personality. Thankfully, as McKnight continues, "But some of the most significant leaders are introverts and are not 'born to lead.'"[3] Similarly, though introverted, people in my immediate circles saw me as a leader. In due course, I found myself serving in various leadership positions—for example, being elected as the president of my class both junior and senior years of high school.

In the bulk of the leadership speech on that brisk, fall evening, I articulated what I believed leadership to be: Leadership is most effective when leaders exhibit humility and service. However, the art of leadership implies far more than my simplistic definition suggests. When you walk into any bookstore, you'll notice the sheer volume of books written on the topic of leadership. Both secular and Christian experts on leadership have put forth their definitions for what a leader is and what he or she does to influence others.

This lesson focuses on the role of pastor as leader. How does one develop as a pastoral leader? And what does it mean to lead a church? By the end of this lesson, I hope that every pastor will see herself as a leader and reap some practical tools to become an effective leader to shepherd and lead one's congregation.

Pastors Are Called to Lead

There is a profound shortage of leaders in churches across North America though there is not a shortage of literature on leadership.[4] The crux of the problem is that many pastors don't know where to begin in real-life ministry. Rowland Forman, Jeff Jones, and Bruce Miller observe, "Most churches are strapped for good leadership and have no intentional strategy for

---

2. McKnight, *Pastor Paul*, 25.

3. McKnight, *Pastor Paul*, 25.

4. In 2020 alone, there have been several books written on Christian leadership. See, for example, Daley, *Gravitas*; Ells, *Resilient Leader*; Henderson, *Glorious Finish*; Lake, *Multiplication Effect*; Sanchez, *Leadership Formula*; Small, *Leader in You*; Smith, *Wisdom from Babylon*; Tripp, *Lead*; and Vanderbloemen and Bird, *Next*.

developing leaders. Even many pastors feel ill-equipped, sensing that their training has not given them the competencies they need to be effective in their role."[5] Glenn Daman concurs, "It doesn't take long for most pastors to realize there is much they are still not equipped to deal with. They may have arrived at their churches, thinking that all they need to do is provide exegetically sound sermons relevant to the needs of the people, but it soon becomes evident that the role of pastor involves much more."[6]

In a time where pastors of larger congregations have become specialists rather than generalists, the church has deferred leadership training to those who know how to manage personalities. We have cleverly titled such persons executive pastors. More often than not, executive pastors relate more closely to being a corporate executive than serving the body of Christ as a pastoral shepherd in the traditional sense. With such designated titles, churches have forgotten that all pastors are leaders. Ed Stetzer and Mike Dodson comment, "Leadership is about influence. Churches that are in a pattern of plateau or decline need strong leaders who will point the way to revitalization."[7] As a pastoral leader, we set the tone for the entire church. We are expected to have a clear vision or road map for the congregation to follow.

Establish Your Vision (over Time)

A clear vision is critical to the survival and success of any organization. Vision is "a clear, shared, and compelling picture of the preferred future to which God is calling the congregation."[8] Churches place much significance on a pastor's vision or lack thereof. The topic of vision is one of the first questions asked by pastoral search committees. John Maxwell states, "Vision is everything for a leader. It is utterly indispensable. . . . Show me a leader without vision, and I'll show you someone who isn't going anywhere. At best, he is traveling in circles."[9] Vision is important because it provides purpose and allows us to prioritize our programs, events, time, and resources. In any church, the pursuit of trendy programs can be limitless. We can take the church down myriad avenues and rabbit trails. But a

5. Forman et al., *Leadership Baton*, 24.

6. Daman, *Leading the Small Church*, 82.

7. Stetzer and Dodson, "Producing a Comeback Church," 38.

8. Herrington et al., *Leading Congregational Change*, 50.

9. Maxwell, *21 Indispensable Qualities*, 150.

clear vision enables us to concentrate on only the things that expand that central vision.

Every church's vision should be to glorify God. At our core, we are all seeking to improve our lives as Jesus' disciples. The questions are how will we do that, and in what areas do we require additional growth?

It's important to note that leadership in ministry is not equivalent to leadership in the business world. Skye Jethani observes, "Many of us in ministry are drawn to the strategies tested and proven by leaders of secular corporations because they are the most celebrated and successful leaders in our culture."[10] But the overall vision of the church should embody the passions that God has laid on leaders' hearts and not just pragmatic strategies that may yield numeric growth. Numeric growth alone is not what glorifies God—despite what the world tells us. What matters is that we are receiving, adopting, and living out God's vision for our local church.

I think it's naive to tell your church what their vision should be in the first year of ministry. Why? We haven't been around long enough to know the unique set of challenges within the church and its surroundings. We don't know the visions that pastoral leaders have pursued in our church's past. Our opinion is important, but it is only one of numerous voices in the body of Christ. So the creation of a congregational vision ought to be a joint pursuit.

I heard of a gifted young pastor whose church had grown stagnant over a period of years prior to his arrival. Rather than soliciting the opinions of his church leaders, the young pastor outlined on his own accord what the future steps of the church would be. He didn't last long enough to see that vision through. Take the necessary time to learn about the church, its history, its leaders, and its passions before goading them in a new direction. Make the creation of the church's vision a collective effort.

Before I arrived onto the scene, one church I served had a two-tiered vision. One tier was to become a multiethnic congregation—having a membership of various ethnicities and cultures. To accommodate this vision, the previous senior pastor enforced a rule that nobody could speak in a language other than English or eat ethnic food during the lunch fellowship. This gesture of removing other languages and cultures was an attempt to accommodate everyone. As time went on, many parishioners expressed how they went along with this multiethnic vision, because that's what the senior pastor wanted. However, the lay leaders didn't take ownership of

10. Jethani, *Immeasurable*, 11.

the vision, and it eventually waned. In short, there was no buy-in from the leaders or from the wider congregation. While ethnic and cultural diversity increased during my time there, I eventually left a predominantly Korean American church with some whites, Chinese Americans, Vietnamese Americans, and a few others.

A second major vision was to support overseas missions. I was, of course, in favor of this vision concerning missions as it's an imperative of Jesus Christ. God's heart is to bring the gospel message to the nations. So the congregation supported foreign missionaries as well as went on several short-term mission trips. In general, missions was a central value of the church and I hope this never stops.

Yet there is a difference between a general vision for all Christian churches and a unique church vision of what makes a congregation distinct from any other church. Every church is expected to evangelize. Every church is commanded to make disciples. Every church should study and know the word of God. Every church should support local and global missions. Every church should care for widows, orphans, and the disenfranchised. And there are other common visions for Christian churches.

But what's difficult in the first year or two is figuring out what the unique vision of your church is. Who are you called to minister to? How does your church make an impact on your neighborhood and community? How does your congregation work with local government? What should you spend your time and financial resources on? In your first year or two, pray with your leaders for a lucid vision of how your church can contribute to the work of building God's kingdom. Wait for God to communicate his vision in his time. And when God leads your church down a concrete path, move prayerfully toward it together. Rowland Forman and his colleagues agree with this strategy of developing a collective vision for the church:

> Lately a number of writers have proposed a model of vision crafting in which the pastor "hears" from God a vision for the church and then presents it to the leadership team to adopt and implement. We believe this model of unilateral leadership is flawed. Our experience has confirmed that a collaborative approach in which key leaders work together as a team will deliver better results. The pastor may be facilitating and leading the process, but the whole team is involved from the beginning.[11]

11. Forman et al., *Leadership Baton*, 136.

This shared approach to creating a church vision does not mean pastors fail to exercise leadership. We don't lead per se as backseat drivers. In fact, as ministers, we need a resurgence of audacity in the pastorate. We need to salvage and strengthen our backbones. John Galloway, Jr. has striking comments about the lack of courage among some pastors. He states,

> If I had but one observation it would be that we have become a bunch of chickens. We hassle and whine and manipulate, often making a big deal of minor issues. We do not seem to have the courage to lead on the issues that matter most. As a group, we in the clergy do not have a compelling sense of vision. We have lost the capacity to dream about what is possible. We have given up on our own ministry and congregation, becoming content with lack of commitment, assuming this is how it is these days. We just find it safer not to dream dreams. We play career games. We lie to one another. We serve on boards. We strut at denominational gatherings. And our churches just stay the same old same old.[12]

Instead, God is calling this new generation of pastors to an exciting life of exercising leadership and exploring grand visions. May we dream with gusto as God reveals his specific plans for our lives and our churches.

Lead Your Pastoral Staff

If you are blessed with a pastoral team, demonstrating wise leadership is paramount. Whether this ministry team is made up of two members or ten, there are principles to be garnered for effective team leadership. While solo pastors have their own set of challenges, directing a pastoral staff invites other unanticipated scenarios and conflicts. Like King Solomon, we must ask God for an extra dose of wisdom.

Developing a pastoral leadership team takes time and much face-to-face interaction. Gene Getz met every single week for two hours at a time with his pastoral staff. In this process, he demonstrated how leadership training was a central priority in his weekly schedule.[13]

While I started on my own, our small congregation of less than a hundred adult members was blessed to eventually have three pastors. After a few years, we had a full-time associate/worship pastor, a part-time youth minister, and me. We possessed different gifts and complemented

12. Galloway, Jr., *Ministry Loves Company*, 2–3.
13. Forman et al., *Leadership Baton*, 39.

each other well. We initially met together twice per month. One meeting focused on the logistics of church life. We took inventory of what was visibly happening at church. We brainstormed and planned together for upcoming events. We critiqued the church's strengths and weaknesses. And we tried to figure out ways to improve the worship service and the overall health and spirit of the church.

The second meeting was designated for accountability and spiritual formation. We prayed together for the church and for our individual lives and shared our personal struggles with one another. This latter meeting was crucial for camaraderie and trust. I cherished this time to be vulnerable with fellow servant leaders. Over time, we found that meeting biweekly was insufficient. We weren't able to cover every topic in depth as we would have liked or even needed. For this reason, we met weekly, alternating each week's agenda as mentioned previously.

Practically speaking, how can we effectively lead our pastoral staff? Like every ministry in the life of a church, prayer is indispensable in building a pastoral team. Be vigilant in setting aside time to pray with your fellow pastors. Pray not only for your respective duties but also for each other's personal and family lives. Without prayer, we lose sight of God, and our personal agendas can take over. Countless churches have divided over the inability of the senior pastor and associate pastors to maintain a healthy, growing relationship.[14] The evil one wants members of the pastoral staff to bicker and collide on various matters. At one church, a worship arts pastor and a student ministries pastor no longer speak to each other because "they are jealous and competitive and mistrustful."[15] Prayer is one of the only weapons we have to preserve unity and tranquility among the pastoral leadership.

Second, remember to communicate and reinforce the vision of the church to each pastoral staff member regularly. In staff meetings, crystallize the vision and see how the staff can best articulate that vision to the rest of the congregation through its sermons, corporate worship, small groups, and other venues. A friend of mine who serves on the staff of a large church shared how his senior pastor asked the staff to read through a book together on vision, which helped get the entire pastoral team on the same page. These discussions have solidified the church's vision and alleviated confusion. That's one way to do it. Since vision drives the church, the pastoral team needs to embrace and disseminate that objective to the whole body.

14. See Bonem and Patterson, *Leading from the Second Chair*.
15. Bonem and Patterson, *Leading from the Second Chair*.

Third, to maximize effectiveness as a pastoral team, identify each person's role in the ministry, which will prevent redundancy. While there may be overlap in certain areas like pastoral care or administration, frequently discuss the unique responsibilities of each team member. For instance, to share the load in teaching Bible studies, our pastoral staff worked according to a scheduled rotation. Each person knew when he or she would teach on a given day, way in advance. At the same time, we had individual duties that reflected our talents, interests, and specialties. Knowing what every pastor will contribute each week will help you maximize your efforts. Prepare a calendar for preaching and teaching and divide up accordingly.

Last, create opportunities throughout the year to enjoy one another's company. Ministry can be fun and recreational. Pastors are not exempt from playtime, within parameters. Go out and treat your pastoral team to a good meal. Take an evening to watch a baseball game. Have a cookout. Go see a play or a musical together. Partake in each other's hobbies. Ministry doesn't have to be static. Humor shared among pastors will have intangible and lasting benefits.

Equip Your Lay Leaders

Contrary to popular belief, Jesus never intended for ministry to be a solo effort. The idiom *solo pastor* is a misnomer. Ministry was supposed to be a communal endeavor for the entire body of faith to share in the work of the local church. Sadly, many pastors have succumbed to this erroneous view that he or she is paid by the members to single-handedly keep the church afloat.

While solo ministry was not Jesus' manifesto, the pattern is often difficult to break in parish life. As discussed in lesson 3, pastoral responsibilities are copious. We often fall prey to what the late Charles Hummel called "the tyranny of the urgent."[16] We work on what is most pressing on our schedules: preparing the Sunday sermon and Bible studies, caring for parishioners, getting the bulletin ready, and attending to other congregational crises. What often gets pushed aside is building up our leaders and equipping the saints.

R. Paul Stevens exhorts, "Equipping is not a gift that some people have and others do not. Rather, it is what each of us is called to do with the gift

16. Hummel, *Tyranny of the Urgent*, 6.

for ministry he or she has."[17] To be effective, learn to develop leaders and delegate responsibility. A growing concern that I've seen in recent years is that leaders are not cognizant of people's strengths and weaknesses. A person is often given responsibility in a ministry area in which he or she is simply not gifted. It may seem like a kind gesture to "promote" someone, but it's not the best use of his or her time and talents. Sometimes, ambition gets in the way and people nod yes to positions that they shouldn't have. I've seen it in the church and in the seminary context too many times. I strongly encourage you to refrain from putting people in improper roles. It hurts the church, the individual, and his or her family. Proper delegation means giving responsibilities to people who are talented and interested in said work. It also means waiting to delegate responsibilities until we have a solid grasp of people and their abilities. As pastors, delegation involves differentiating what is imperative for us to do and discerning what is optional.

One of the major obstacles facing any new pastor is lay leadership training. In fact, many seminaries do not offer courses on leadership skills. When I started at my church, some of the core members offered their well-meaning suggestions. They said, "Please focus your attention on the fringe members." I listened to their counsel. In the first few months, I called those on the membership directory and contacted those on the outskirts of the church. While this effort was valuable in bringing some floaters and skeptics back to the church, I failed to develop existing leaders. In short, I didn't equip the saints for the ministry.

As a young pastor, I learned from my many mistakes in lay leadership development. While I still met with those on the periphery, I was intentional in meeting with our church's core leadership. Again, our model for leadership is Jesus. He built relationships and partnerships with a small nucleus of followers, the twelve disciples. Among those twelve, he focused particularly on three individuals: Peter, James, and John. Jesus did not exert all his energy and resources on the crowd. That's the gaffe that I made early on in that pastorate.

Why is it so important that we build up lay leaders apart from the obvious in sharing the workload? First, it is crucial that we leave a permanent legacy in our churches. Aubrey Malphurs and Will Mancini convey the following:

> The challenge is to recruit and develop godly emerging leaders. This is our ministry legacy. When God takes us home, we

17. Stevens, *Liberating the Laity*, 110.

want people to remember us for the number of godly, competent leaders who are in Christ-honoring ministries around the world because we made leadership development a priority in our busy ministry schedules.[18]

In other words, the church should be able to thrive without us. That is the proper test of whether or not we have produced quality lay leaders.

The Apostle Paul offers a second important reason for leadership formation in his analogy to the Christians in Corinth. The local church is a body made up of many different parts. God doesn't give every skill set to one pastor. No, he chooses to diversify his portfolio of talents, scattering abilities to every person in the life of the church. We become aware rather quickly of the things that we're not good at or don't enjoy. With prayer and discernment, pass that responsibility on to someone else who can flourish by exercising her God-given gifts. Remember, you were never meant to be all and do all.

Hazards of Leadership

While being a leader has its definite upsides, leadership has its share of pitfalls as well. I'd like to draw our attention to three of those imminent hazards: conflict, criticism, and sometimes being companionless.

Embrace Conflict

Conflict is usually unavoidable when people are involved. How we deal with conflict, however, will display our leadership ability and may govern our ministry longevity. Instead of addressing conflict, pastors often deflect it or hope that it will subside on its own. We live with the axiom that "time heals all wounds." These options only suppress the problem and do not resolve issues at their core. For effective leadership to ensue in the pastorate, pastors must learn to handle conflict well.

Not everyone in the local church family is a team player. People can be self-interested, wanting things to go their way. People in your church may manipulate certain individuals to assume power over a social group or a particular ministry. Some people seek to control the pastor by playing the role

18. Malphurs and Mancini, *Building Leaders*, 28.

of puppeteer. Before difficult situations arise, it's beneficial to think through how you might deal with a crisis of interpersonal conflict.

In their premarital counseling book *Preparing for Marriage*, David Boehi and his colleagues describe four typical ways married couples respond to conflict. The first is the attitude of fighting to win. According to this position, "you seek to dominate the other person; personal relationships take second place to the need to triumph."[19] Stated differently, you'll do or say anything just to win that battle, even if it emotionally destroys the one you love.

The second way to approach conflict is to withdraw from the situation. Rather than meeting the conflict head on, this tactic causes a person to retreat to his or her room and avoids the conversation altogether. He or she may give their spouse the "silent treatment" by emotionally leaving for a period of time.[20]

Third, a husband or wife may yield to the other's wishes. This type of conflict resolution says, "Rather than starting another argument, whatever you wish is fine."[21] Men often have a tendency to resort to saying sorry just to pacify a heated argument. Nothing gets resolved in the end.

The final option is to resolve conflict by discussing the issues. Here, the mentality is, "You value your relationship more than winning or losing, escaping or feeling comfortable."[22] How we deal with conflict in a marriage relationship parallels conflict resolution among God's people. As pastors, it makes sense that implementing option four is most effectual from a biblical standpoint. In many circumstances, we should err on the side of preserving church unity in conflict scenarios. How do you tend to deal with conflict?

Embrace Criticism

A necessary trait in being the face of a local church body is the ability to embrace criticism. It just comes with the territory. Notice I didn't say we should love criticism or even like it. But we must come to grips with the fact that we'll hear our share of criticism as pastors and, though difficult,

---

19. Boehi et al., *Preparing for Marriage*, 147.
20. Boehi et al., *Preparing for Marriage*, 147.
21. Boehi et al., *Preparing for Marriage*, 148.
22. Boehi et al., *Preparing for Marriage*, 148.

we must learn to love our critics. Not everyone will like us or appreciate us. We need to be okay with that.

My seminary mentor once told me that usually it's not us (pastors) that church members dislike but rather what we stand for. The biblical principles we espouse and disseminate as ministers usually fly in the face of suspicious younger generations, while older generations typically don't like change.[23] They don't want to be told how to live, especially by someone who they think doesn't really understand them or by someone who could be their grandchild. Leighton Ford writes in *Transforming Leadership*, "The parable of the tenants in the vineyard is really Jesus' autobiography, and it gives us an insight into what it means to be a leader who is rejected. God's servants may find their authority not only questioned, but actually resisted—painfully, shamefully, even fatally."[24]

On occasion the criticism thrown our way is valid. Perhaps we didn't follow through on a promise we made, and it becomes hard to live down. We're forever seen as an oath breaker. Instead of taking time to listen to another's point of view, perhaps we spoke too quickly only to later eat our words. From that point onward, we are regarded as foolish and unwise. Criticism is at times warranted because of our humanity and our foibles.

Yet there may be moments in our ministry where our parishioners are simply seeking to pick a fight and we become their target. To rehash a simple well-known truth, not every church member will like us or support what we do. There will always be a faction (hopefully a small one) that will not endorse us, our teaching, or our plans for the ministry. We can't allow the naysayers to paralyze us. Embrace their criticism for what it is, and decipher how you can improve on your areas of weakness. Find people who you trust and ask them for wisdom on how you can develop as a leader.

Embrace Being Companionless

A third aspect of leadership that comes with the territory is loneliness. Leaders, especially pastoral leaders, are often lonely. Robert Putnam shed much light on this topic in *Bowling Alone*. In it, he describes the penchant of Americans to be isolated from others. He contends that American society as a whole has become disengaged and has lost its sense of community.[25] I've experienced overtones of this attitude in my own neighborhood where

23. See Sbanotto and Blomberg, *Effective Generational Ministry*.

24. Ford, *Transforming Leadership*, 264.

25. Putnam, *Bowling Alone*, 19.

people seldom acknowledge each other. Instead, we quickly dart up the driveway, pull into our garages, close the garage door behind us, and hope that nobody saw us. Many people just don't want to be bothered.

Even though people surround us throughout the week, pastors feel lonely for a number of reasons. Some pastors experience loneliness because we're so preoccupied with work that we forget to build new relationships and fight to keep the friendships that we once cherished. Others are so busy caring for congregants that they are stretched too thin to interact with members of the outside world. Another type of pastor finds comfort in sheltering himself from the insecurity wrought by neighboring pastors so he only travels within the petite dimensions of his study at home or church. The most dangerous form of loneliness arises from the Lone Ranger mentality, where one is revered by many for being a hero, but he is accountable to no one.

Though we embrace loneliness to an extent, we are called to forge friendships with others. As discussed in the preceding lesson, friends are hard to come by. They are more elusive the older we get. Make it your ambition to cultivate friendships wherever you can. Maybe you'll meet someone at the fitness center or at a school PTA meeting. Befriend a pastor down the street irrespective of your theological leanings. Grow a stronger bond with your spouse if you're married. The evil one wants us to feel alone and unloved. Being a leader invites loneliness, but becoming more proactive can assuage it.

Lead as Jesus Did

Jesus was not the CEO of a lucrative, global enterprise. But he knew how to lead others well. In his three productive years of ministry, Jesus led his disciples based on his Father's will. At every turn, Jesus prayed and asked his Father what he should do. If we're honest with ourselves, we need God's assistance to lead our churches effectively. If we want to lead like Jesus, we must follow in his footsteps.

In *The Monkey and the Fish*, Dave Gibbons suggests a leadership principle taken from a rather unlikely source, the late martial artist Bruce Lee. In one interview Lee observes, "You put water into a cup, it becomes the cup. You put water in the bottle, it becomes the bottle. You put it into a teapot and it becomes a teapot. The water can flow. The water can crash. Be water, my friend."[26] Gibbons suggests that Jesus became water to a dying and thirsty world. He adapted his approach in how he communicated

26. Gibbons, *Monkey and the Fish*, 92–93.

to and cared for lost souls. Gibbons maintains that the church "is in need of adaptive and contextualized language and forms when talking about God and Christianity."[27] Yet in adapting to his listeners and followers, Jesus didn't lose his boldness, character, or heart of service.

Jesus Led with Boldness

In the Gospels, Jesus is the quintessential leader. He instructed his disciples on how to live a righteous, God-honoring life. He never shied away from conflict. He didn't shrink when the religious leaders accused him of sinning against the Torah. No, Jesus was bold, and his boldness eventually rubbed off on his disciples. Remember the transformation that took place in Peter and John through the empowerment of the Holy Spirit? They became so emboldened even to declare, "As for us, we cannot help speaking about what we have seen and heard" (Acts 4:20).

To lead in the twenty-first century, we must reclaim the boldness of Jesus. Do we truly believe in God's mission and his plan to redeem creation? Will we act boldly in response to God's call? Are we willing to suffer and even die for the cause of Christ? Are we standing up for biblical morality and biblical principles? Are we losing sleep to intercede for the flock? Are we relinquishing earthly desires to be used by God?

Jesus didn't make any apologies for obeying his father's commands. He simply obeyed even when challenged by the leaders of the social and religious establishments. As pastors, we must lead our congregations with boldness and tenacity. We must be willing to put our necks out for the sake of doctrinal truth and not crumble when skeptics try to subdue our faith. Like Jesus, my prayer is that this rising generation of pastors will influence their sheep with confidence, not timidity. And I hope our congregants will see many examples where their spiritual leader did not back down from life's challenges, but rather with God's help broke spiritual strongholds and fought on behalf of justice, the lost, and the least among us.

Jesus Led with Character

Before Jesus began his earthly ministry, the Holy Spirit sent him on an excursion to the desert. He was hungry and exhausted, having not eaten

27. Gibbons, *Monkey and the Fish*, 93.

in forty days. Satan approached him in his time of weakness and offered him three basic human desires: food to alleviate his hunger, the wealth and power of the world at his disposal, and safety from physical harm.

In each of these temptations, Jesus wards off Satan's bait with the promises found in God's word. Jesus didn't give into Satan's pressure. And in this battle for his soul, Jesus triumphs and commences his ministry with pristine character. He will conclude in precisely the same fashion. It is said, "Your ideal is what you wish you were. Your reputation is what people say you are. Your character is what you are."[28] As a leader, Jesus modeled character for his followers. As pastors, we can't overestimate the importance of godly character. It's so important that I'm going to circle back to this issue in a bonus lesson (Lesson 7.1). It sticks to us wherever we go, and those who follow behind can feel the difference between a genuine bill and a fake.

As Jesus lived his final days on earth, what kept the disciples attracted to the mission was Jesus' character. He was faithful and kept his word at all times. He didn't take shortcuts in life. He didn't allow his heart to lust after women or the enticing things of this world. He wouldn't crumble on those recurring exams of his integrity. In this age of loose morality, we need pastors with strong character not just when we're in front of people but also in the quietness of our cars, offices, homes, and backyards. May we lead like Jesus and lead with character that can never be taken away.

Jesus Led with Service

Although Jesus did his share of educating his followers about sacrificial living and the call to discipleship, we see numerous examples of Jesus serving others. The primary example, of course, comes on the evening of the Passover meal where Jesus removes the towel from his waist and washes his disciples' feet. There are few greater demonstrations of servanthood than that foot-washing ceremony.

In *How Would Jesus Raise a Child?*, Teresa Whitehurst observes, "Jesus served his disciples by teaching and carefully modeling servant leadership, rather than using a command-and-control model or leaving them to their own devices. He went to a lot of trouble to help them develop their leadership skills because he had such high hopes for them. Jesus knew that service is the path to influence."[29] More than blasting out imperatives, a pastor's humble

28. Green, *Illustrations for Biblical Preaching*, 39.
29. Whitehurst, *How Would Jesus Raise a Child?*, 57.

service to her people speaks louder than her words. When we serve our parishioners, they will be more willing to listen. After the corporate worship service each Sunday, our church members shared a meal together. Before I became the senior pastor, there were glaring problems with clean-up duties after the meal. By default, one of the leaders took it upon himself to tidy up the fellowship hall every Sunday. Nobody got up to assist him.

My father always told me that people will participate in something when the pastor models that behavior first. From the outset of my ministry, I cleaned the church. No, this wasn't in my job description, but it was absolutely necessary to break negative, long-standing cleaning rituals. Congregants expressed their surprise the first month or so and even asked, "Matt, you're the senior pastor, why are you cleaning?" And I responded, "I'm cleaning because I'm the pastor." Eventually, one by one other people took ownership of cleaning the church. It all started because the senior pastor chose to serve rather than be served. Our humble service is critical for people to notice that their pastor is willing to get his hands dirty, and hopefully they'll follow the leader.

We don't become leaders overnight. That's the good news. In the course of becoming a leader, we will most likely fail more than we succeed. The example above is one moment where I got it right. However, as we trust God and seek his will through prayer, leadership skills will materialize in us. Part of learning to become a pastor requires learning to become a leader. Leadership skills don't spring upon us suddenly with chronological age. It's a reflection of how we live our lives whether we are twenty-five or sixty-five. If we lead like Jesus, with boldness, character, and service, our congregants will put faith in our leadership and collectively trek toward the path of Christ and his kingdom.

Ask Yourself

1. What is my definition of leadership?

2. Do I consider myself a leader, and why or why not?

3. How do I deal with conflict, criticism, and loneliness?

4. How can I sharpen my leadership skills?

6

Love Your Congregation

Ministry is People

My MENTOR IN SEMINARY described being a pastor with three simple words: "Ministry is people." That's good news for some and bad news for others. But if we keep this tenet close to our hearts, we will find greater satisfaction in ministry and injure fewer sheep along the way. Although ministers perform countless responsibilities in church life, a love for people is indispensable. Future pastoral leaders often enter seminary because they were once shown God's love by someone, and they want to proliferate that experience for others. But something can happen over the course of a seminary career where that initial love for people gets pushed aside for the quest of theological ideas and religious ideologies.

During seminary training, many of my classmates would engage in lengthy discussions about the use of Hebrew syntax or chew over irresolvable theological mysteries. These intellectual conversations piqued their interest because many had the impression that the accumulation of knowledge was the primary goal of ministry. Don't get me wrong: Seminarians should pursue scholarship vigorously by examining the Bible and digging deeply into theology and related subjects. However, it saddens me that I can only remember a handful of conversations where my fellow seminarians discussed the stuff of real life: the joys and struggles of living, breathing people. Sometimes, as I walk across campus, there are students who will not even say hello when greeted. They keep their eyes glued to the pavement and walk right by. Friendliness is not a given just because God has called us into pastoral work. It doesn't always come naturally for many. Friendliness and love for others requires intentionality.

Having pivoted from the pastorate to the professorate in 2012, I continue to see that pedagogies of theological education are all over the map in terms of people-orientation. If you glance at the Association of Theological Schools' website,[1] you can visit seminaries virtually and learn about their required courses, such as the Master of Divinity degree. In degrees historically geared toward the pastorate, such as the MDiv degree, certain seminaries, as they should, prescribe heavy doses of classical theological courses, such as: Hebrew, Greek, Old and New Testament exegesis, hermeneutics, church history, and theology. However, there is a disproportionately reduced number of required practical theology courses—like leadership, counseling, pastoral care, conflict, evangelism and discipleship, Christian education (is that even offered anymore?), and preaching.

On the other hand, some institutions, seeking to broaden the appeal and affordability of a seminary education through shorter degree programs, minimize both sides of the theological seminary equation: fewer Bible/theology as well as fewer ministry-oriented courses. Sadly, some quip that many seminaries have catered to the "cheap, quick, and easy" mentality that answers some who may ask: What's the minimum that I can do and still earn a theological degree? Of course, this is not the attitude of all seminarians-to-be, but perhaps it is for some. Sometimes it's one's circumstances while other times it's one's attitude.

As a whole, speaking here to administrators and faculty members, theological seminaries can do better to integrate and synergize Bible, theology, and church history with ministry courses. The church cannot afford to have seminary education be fundamentally about scholarship to the neglect of service. Both are critical to the expansion of God's kingdom. All theological institutions must remember that ministry is about people.[2] We need to train students better to love people and minister effectively to them. Moreover, as I've noted earlier, many seminary professors have very little or no experience as full-time pastors or missionaries. Not to sound overly critical, but pastoring on the side while working full-time as a professor or researching as a doctoral student is not the same as full-time vocational pastoral ministry. When experiential wisdom is lacking in ministering to real people, teaching about ministry is done merely in theory.

1. See Association of Theological Schools, www.ats.edu.
2. Foster et al., *Educating Clergy*, 18.

The office of pastor has changed over the last few decades. To some, the title of pastor refers to an entrepreneur who can guide the church in new directions like a consummate businessperson. To others, pastors are preachers, teachers, counselors, visionaries, or administrators. As such, the numerous hats worn by a pastor often preclude her engaging in what pastors should really aspire to: loving members of the church. This lesson will address the necessity of being a minister who loves others and will offer some proposals for how one can strive toward this goal. I'm one of the first to admit that it's not easy to love others. And yet, as a seminary student or a new pastor, I would encourage you to go back to the basics. Ministry is about people and loving the members of our parishes.

Love is the Greatest Commandment

Love is a biblical concept that is not limited to pastors but applies to all believers in Christ. Yet how much more should love be the motivating factor for those who serve God's people on a full-time basis? Jesus taught us about the centrality of love in the Christian life. For instance, when a teacher of the law approached Jesus and questioned him, "Of all the commandments, which is the most important?" (Mark 12:28), Jesus responded by quoting from the book of Deuteronomy: "'Love the Lord your God with all your heart and with all your soul and with all your mind and with all your strength.'" The second commandment is this, "'Love your neighbor as yourself. There is no commandment greater than these'" (Mark 12:30–31). Jesus equates our love for God with our love for others. The message is clear. When we fail to love others, we naturally fall short in loving our heavenly Father.

The Apostle Paul, in his letters to the Christian churches scattered throughout the Roman empire, similarly described love as being our primary motivation in serving God. He instructed the Thessalonian church that above all things, their labor should be motivated by love (1 Thess 1:3). Additionally, in his illustrious first letter to the Corinthian church, Paul exhorts them to have proper intentions in their expressions of spirituality:

> If I speak in the tongues of men or of angels, but do not have love,
> I am only a resounding gong or a clanging cymbal. If I have the gift
> of prophecy and can fathom all mysteries and all knowledge, and if
> I have a faith that can move mountains, but do not have love, I am
> nothing. If I give all I possess to the poor and give over my body to

hardship that I may boast, but do not have love, I gain nothing. . . .
And now these three remain: faith, hope and love. But the greatest
of these is love. (1 Cor 13:1–3, 13)

Therefore, love is a vital ingredient in our ecclesial mission.

Why is love so critical to the pastoral office? When we truly love someone, it is in our nature to give. We want to spend time with them and share
our resources with them. When we are deficient in love for others, however, pastoral ministry may develop into a painstaking chore rather than a
healthy by-product of affection. The former attitude encourages anger and
resentment, whereas the latter engenders forbearance and generosity. In
order to minister effectively, love is imperative.

Get to Know the Sheep

At the outset of our ministry, it is crucial that we love our congregants by
building healthy relationships with them. Jim Elliff writes, "He [the pastor]
may be concerned for truth; he may be concerned for preaching; he may be
concerned for growth; he may be concerned for evangelism. But if he is not
concerned about the sheep, he is only a hireling."[3]

We authenticate genuine concern for parishioners when we get acquainted with them, their families, their backgrounds, and their life experiences. Why is the process of getting to know our people so important in
pastoral ministry? It is because of the trust factor. People need to be able to
trust their pastor and know that he or she sincerely cares for them. David
Hansen urges, "The great missing element in today's relationships between
pastor and laypeople is trust. Trust comes from love and understanding."[4]

Before we can make any plans for the church, we must know the sheep
well. Take every opportunity to become familiar with members of your
church. Don't rush into your action plans too quickly. At a church my parents
once attended, the new senior pastor in his first year arrived not with a spirit
to love people but rather with a goal to change the status quo. Instead of taking time to establish relationships with his congregants, he sought to make
the church into his own image. He started changing every component of the
church that didn't suit him. What a tragic mistake. After only nine months,

---

3. Elliff, "Cure of Souls," 148.

4. Hansen, *Art of Pastoring*, 12–13.

this new pastor was asked to vacate his position. His actions eventually repulsed the church, and many of the sheep scattered as a result.

Jesus spent a lot of time with people. David Hansen observes, "The New Testament corroborates that Jesus was a friend to sinners. He visited with them on the streets, called them as disciples, attended their parties and invited himself over to their houses for dinner. In friendship Jesus shared the gospel."[5] We build closer connections with our people over extended periods of time. Deep, lasting relationships cannot form merely during the coffee hour on Sunday mornings. Connections emerge when we convene with people both inside and outside of the church walls.

During our first year in that pastorate, my wife and I made a commitment to have one family, married couple, or individual over for dinner each week at the church parsonage. We didn't have children at the time, so it was easier back then. We now have three growing sons whose lives are becoming increasingly active. What we realized quickly, however, is that church people covet the attention of their pastor and the pastor's spouse. They want to feel genuinely loved by us. Having members of the church over to your home for a meal will amplify this sense of rapport with them. Although it can be physically demanding to prepare and host a home-cooked meal regularly, the sacrifice is worth the effort. If you aren't skilled at cooking, order carryout. In this more personal setting, at your residence, your guests will be liberated to share more openly with you than they would in the fellowship hall where others may overhear your conversation. In that first year, we made a strong connection with numerous people in our congregation. Everyone enjoys a good meal. So establish opportunities early on in your ministry to break bread with your church members. Show hospitality (1 Tim 3:2; Titus 1:8; and 1 Pet 4:9).[6]

Another positive way to build relationships is to visit congregants at their workplaces. Jesus went where the people were: to their jobs. For instance, Jesus found Levi by stopping at his tax collector's booth.[7] Jesus also traveled to the Sea of Galilee to initiate a relationship with some fishermen named Simon, Andrew, James, and John (Matt 4:18–22). By visiting a parishioner's store or office, we can get a sense of our congregants' daily life. People want to know that we are interested in them, invested in them, and care about them holistically. Since making money is a significant part

5. Hansen, *Art of Pastoring*, 117.

6. See also Butterfield, *Gospel Comes with a House Key*.

7. Butterfield, *Gospel Comes with a House Key*.

of people's lives, become familiar with what your people do occupationally. Ask questions about their line of work, about their coworkers, and about their joys and struggles on the job.[8] This insight will become valuable in understanding your people.

You can be creative in your calling to know the sheep as well. One pastor built friendships with people in his new pastorate through eating dessert together. Who doesn't enjoy a scrumptious piece of homemade apple pie? Every Saturday evening for two hours the pastor's home was open to visitors from the congregation. Dessert was offered as the pastor and his wife shared life together over an assortment of cakes, pies, and cookies. On Tuesday mornings, members of the church were invited for a coffee hour with the pastor's spouse. Through these types of informal venues, bonds will begin to solidify between your family and members of the flock, and they give us opportunities to listen to their narratives.

Listen to People's Stories

Pastors are often expected to be good communicators, but sometimes we forget that just as important is the art of good listening. It's a skill that fewer people in our society fancy. As an introvert, conversing with people for extended periods fatigues me. I'm not a big talker. Generally, I tend to listen to people more than I talk. In fact, in most scenarios, I spend 90 percent of the time listening to people and speak for less than 10 percent. I'm not one of those people who forces my way into the conversation and cuts others off. That's not my personality. Like other introverted pastors, being alone energizes me. Yet whether we are introverted or extroverted, cultivating our listening skills is a rewarding and even necessary discipline for pastors.

In *Listening Ministry*, Susan Hedahl reminds pastors that the act of listening is a most rudimentary element of communication and a prerequisite for all other forms of ministerial service. She observes, "We all speak frequently and in many ways. But who, after all is said and done, really listens? In fact, we rarely stop to consider the dynamics of listening. Yet listening is the primary trajectory of all other communication acts."[9] She continues, "An inability or refusal to listen could result in death, both spiritual and physical.

8. See Brown, *Sunday's Sermon for Monday's World*.
9. Hedahl, *Listening Ministry*, 2.

It is the life-giving connective link between God and humanity. Yet listening is a communication skill often ignored and little understood."[10]

Many in pastoral ministry would confess that we are better speakers than we are listeners. In the act of speaking, we verbalize our thoughts and opinions to others, whereas in listening we place our ideas on hold. By actively listening, we convey to the person seated in front of us that her thoughts are valuable and that our opinions can wait. If we truly love people as we should, we will make a concerted effort to listen to their life stories.

On one occasion, I had a watershed moment with a particular member of our church through the simple act of listening. Brad shared with me a personal struggle that he couldn't seem to overcome. I'd always had a soft spot for Brad. I knew that he was a loving husband and father who possessed a heart of gold. Yet for whatever reason, he couldn't seem to shake this particular sin in his life.

I had been praying for Brad ever since I became the pastor of that church. Sometimes our listening ministry becomes more than a one-shot deal. I asked Brad if he would meet with me once a week for a couple of hours. He agreed, and we convened at his home every Tuesday for ten weeks. At each of these meetings, Brad disclosed what was in his heart more and more. I didn't need to say much at all. I simply sat and listened to his stories, which were gushing with sentiments of joy and pain.

A year later Brad shared with me how God had done a miracle in his life. Instead of straddling the fence, Brad made the conscious choice to live for God in this thorny area of his life. Through the service of listening, Brad was able to verbalize his problems and receive healing for his wounds. Rather than giving him advice, I was able to extend love by listening. During my time at that church, Brad's faith grew by leaps and bounds. He served faithfully in various ministries of the church with immense joy. He was a new creation in Christ.

Listening is an indispensable part of pastoral ministry. We don't have to feel pressured to relay all the right answers to life's problems. The truth is, we don't have all the answers. Sometimes, all it takes is to open your ears, stay focused, and engage in what others have to say.

10. Hedahl, *Listening Ministry*, 2.

Do Something They Enjoy

Being a pastor involves more than just sitting cooped up in your church study. Although our preparation time is essential, we also love our congregation by meeting with them and participating in their lives. I found that one of the best ways to show church members that I loved them was by doing something they enjoyed.

You may be thinking, "That's all pastors do. Everything we do is for them." Well, let's take the example of the marital relationship. As far as I can tell, marriage is often about personal sacrifice and is focused on our spouse. If we only do things that only one of us enjoys, it probably won't make for a successful marriage. Most likely, my wife will be annoyed and despondent, because her pursuits would be neglected. I demonstrate love for my wife when I partake in her hobbies too.

In a similar way, our congregants feel most appreciated when we participate on their turf. In my first full week in the pastorate, someone who enjoyed wakeboarding asked me to join him and another church member for a morning on the lake. Now, I don't have a penchant for water sports. In fact, I can barely tread water, let alone swim to save my life. However, I blurted out, "Yes, of course, I'll meet you guys." They were very excited for me to share in their most prized form of recreation.

By God's mercy, I was able to get up on the water my first try and even enjoyed thirty seconds of bliss before planting my face in the lake. I ended up swallowing a gallon of water. But doing something at which you're not particularly adept or even interested for the sake of your members is a humbling experience and especially meaningful for them. I gained a valuable lesson that day. Prove to your parishioners that you are invested even in their leisurely activities. That morning, I built a relationship with these brothers in Christ and learned more about them. As time went on, people chuckled at my expense about my wipeouts on the water. Regardless, it was time well spent.

Visit Newborns and the Elderly

Our congregation was relatively young. As a family-oriented church, we were blessed with scores of newborn children. In my first year as pastor, we celebrated the births of more than ten infants. Many congregants joked that we were growing not by evangelism but through conception. In any event, it was a delight to visit families at the hospital.

My wife and I usually phoned first and went to the hospital when both parents were present. We made it our little tradition to bring to first-time parents a calendar that highlighted all landmark moments in the baby's life, such as first words, crawling, walking, and so on. We used this calendar for our sons as well, and it helped us to remember wonderful achievements in their lives. Sometimes, we brought the couple a gift card. However, it's not necessary that you bring anything at all. Your simple presence is greatly appreciated.

After chatting with the couple for a little while, I held the newborn and offered a prayer of blessing on her behalf. I also interceded for the mother, asking God to provide her with a swift recovery. Finally, I requested that God bless the entire family and make the transition as smooth as possible for the entire household.

Visiting the new infant's unit at the hospital was one of my preferred things to do as a pastor. I frequented the hospital almost once a month because of new births. It gave me a unique opportunity to share in my parishioners' joy. Our presence communicated a resemblance of Christlike love in their lives. So I encourage you to visit the hospital whenever a new child joins your church family and bless the family with the love of Jesus.

A second important group you may anticipate dropping in on is the elderly, whether they live at home, in a nursing facility, or in the geriatric wing of a hospital. Ministering to a younger generation, I didn't often have the privilege of loving the aged as a distinct faith community. However, the church whose building we rented was comprised primarily of older parishioners. Every Sunday, between our worship services, I conversed with many of them. Even in those brief interactions, I learned from their life experiences, and they received the warmth of a youthful minister.

When meeting with an elderly person or any other church member at their home, Derek Prime suggests that pastoral visits remain on the shorter side. He writes, "Unless it is a first visit, I reckon half an hour to be the ideal length of time, except when an important matter arises in the conversation that demands to be talked through there and then. . . . It is always better that people should feel our visit is too short than too long."[11] But it is at your full discretion to spend enough quality time with your congregants so that they don't feel shortchanged. Ask them what their schedule is like and proceed

11. Prime and Begg, *On Being a Pastor*, 174–75.

accordingly. Some people may really enjoy your company and expect you to stay awhile. In that case, don't rush off too quickly.

If you are visiting an elderly person who is critically ill, it may be helpful to meet more recurrently for only a few minutes rather than exhaust the patient with a prolonged visit.[12] You may feel that it's an unwise use of your time to spend only a few moments with that person considering the long commute. But keep in mind, we "may be overstaying our privilege and may weary the patient who will be too courteous to tell you."[13] If time permits, pass on a verse of Scripture with an elderly person who is unwell to encourage him or her for the week ahead. Pray with them and ask them to pray out loud, too, if they're able.

As a pastor, you feel obligated to be at everyone's beck and call. Frankly, there are times when you just don't have the energy or even feel like going. However, people want us around in times of celebration and despair. Love your congregation by visiting them in all circumstances. They will appreciate your time and effort even if the gratitude is unspoken. And more importantly, God will recall our sacrifices in ministry and will reward us for being loving shepherds.

Be Available When People Need You Most

Anthony was a name that I heard often, but he hadn't come to church since my arrival. On Thanksgiving Sunday, however, I met Anthony for the first time. Following the service, several of us sat down in the common area to chat. Quite unexpectedly, Anthony began asking me about the hypocrisy he observed among well-known pastors. The tone in his voice indicated a slight hostility. I knew that I was in for an interesting conversation. I tried to answer his questions the best I could. He seemed skeptical about Christianity in general and pastors in particular.

For the next several months, Anthony came to church occasionally. I greeted him warmly every time I saw him. He mattered to me. One afternoon, Anthony called me at home. I just sat and listened. He shared how his mother had passed away and that he didn't know anyone else who could perform the funeral. He asked, "Will you do it?" I accepted his request. Later that week, I went to Anthony's home and met with him and his stepfather. Anthony shared with me about his mother's life and what she meant to him.

12. Prime and Begg, *On Being a Pastor*, 179.

13. Prime and Begg, *On Being a Pastor*, 179.

He explained how he wanted the funeral to be conducted. With this information, I performed the service with respect and sensitivity.

Upon walking alongside of him through this tragedy, something in Anthony changed. He started attending church more consistently. His posture toward me became more amiable. Anthony took opportunities to integrate his family into the life of the church community. Eventually, he and his wife faithfully attended a small group Bible study, and he led one of our church's ministries. Their lives flipped upside down for the better.

At one summer retreat, Anthony pulled me aside and said,

> Hey, Matt, remember when you said in one of your sermons how you wanted to bring hundreds and thousands of people to heaven? Well, I don't know how you define success as a pastor, but I'm a testimony of your love and commitment to this church. This is my first retreat ever, and it's the first time that my wife and I have ever gone to a Bible study. I want you to know that I think you had something to do with that.

With those kind words, tears formed in my eyes. It was the first time I had realized what ministry was all about: We need to love people when they need us most. We represent Jesus Christ to our church family. By our showing them that they are valuable, they will develop a more intimate relationship with God.

Every once in a while, I wonder what would have happened to Anthony had I refused his request. As pastors, the temptation is always there to come up with an excuse not to be there. We may decline someone's petition with the words, "Sorry, I'm just too busy this week" or "Could you please find someone else to do it?" In general, our sheep depend on us to get them through the deep valleys of life. And we are compelled to give our best effort to deliver on their behalf. That's how we love God's church.

Love Difficult People

In every congregation, there will be at least one person who tries your patience. God created no two people alike. Each living being possesses idiosyncrasies that will not be endearing to all. There are some people whom we like and others whom we dislike—yes, even as ministers of the gospel. And, for whatever reason, some people will not like us either.

William Smith paints a portrait of such unpleasant souls in *How to Love Difficult People*:

Some of them are determined to protect themselves; prickly and constantly on the defensive, it only takes something little to set them off. They lash out verbally, and then withdraw emotionally and sometimes physically, cutting off all chance of communication. Others are just plain nasty for no apparent reason. They seem to take perverse pleasure in sabotaging every interaction, so most exchanges end unhappily with hard feelings on both sides. And then there are the Eeyore types who mope through life always looking at the dark side. They notice and (endlessly!) discuss every gloomy detail of their lives. They throw a wet blanket on every conversation. Frankly, I get tired of them all.[14]

Difficult people conceal themselves behind various masks. According to Judson Edwards, author of *The Leadership Labyrinth*, some individuals are relatively harmless, but they tend to drain a pastor emotionally. He states, "The Drainers have an unspoken agenda for me (at least unspoken to me), and I always get the feeling when I'm around them that I'm not quite measuring up, that I've inadvertently failed them."[15] Other more toxic individuals plot the demise of their pastors. G. Lloyd Rediger labels them "clergy killers." He writes, "One informed estimate indicates that a pastor is 'fired' (forced out) every six minutes in the United States. This is a shocking figure, even for those who have been dealing with abuse and conflict in organized religion for many years. Clergy killers are few in number, but awesome in the damage they create."[16]

When dealing with obstinate people, we can react in one of several ways. First, we may retaliate and, in doing so, let them know who's really in charge. Second, we can choose to get under their skin by ignoring them and their requests. Third, rather than allowing such persons to curtail our ministry longevity, we can learn to embrace the good in them and love them with the love of Christ. In all respects, pastors must be shrewd in how we handle distraught folks.

A helpful way I inaugurated the process of loving difficult people was to ask two underlying questions about human experience: "Why is this person like this?" and "What has taken place in this person's life that has made him/her this way?" Once we diagnose the source of the problem, we can administer the prescription of God's grace. Their peculiarities won't agitate us as much. And we won't do or say something that we'll later regret.

14. Smith, *How to Love Difficult People*, 3.
15. Edwards, *Leadership Labyrinth*, 11.
16. Rediger, *Clergy Killers*, 6–7.

When I was in high school, I served as the praise team leader at my church. A female vocalist annoyed me a great deal. She was one of those people that just rubbed everyone the wrong way. During one practice session, she asked, "Matt, it seems like you've improved on the guitar. Have you been practicing?" The sin of pride erupted in me, and I exploded, "Why do you ask? Do you think I was terrible before?" And for the next several minutes I berated her in front of the entire worship team. Nancy began to sob and left the worship practice, never to return.

What I discovered later on through her cousin was that Nancy struggled deeply with insecurity. Growing up, she didn't have many close friends. She liked to kiss up to others, because it helped her get on people's good side. Nancy praised me probably knowing that I wasn't all that fond of her. She thought her benevolent words would pacify our tension-filled relationship. My actions that day were inexcusable and unbecoming of a leader. Perhaps, if I understood her past, I might not have reacted the way I did. I've taken this lesson to heart and try to understand why people are the way they are and give them the benefit of the doubt.

In their book *Lead Like Jesus*, Ken Blanchard and Phil Hodges provide helpful advice on mimicking Jesus' love. They write, "Jesus spent significant time interacting in positive ways with people who disagreed with Him. He did not isolate Himself from those who disagreed; He embraced those who disagreed. He did not change His message to gain approval, but He continued to love those who did not accept His message."[17] The worst thing we can do as ministers is ostracize the ones who don't adhere to our leadership style. That's one of the grave difficulties in pastoral ministry. We are called to love even those whose company we don't enjoy. Win them over to your side through acts of love and charity.

The Burdensome Joy of Ministry

In *The Burdensome Joy of Preaching*, the late James Earl Massey describes the intense heaviness of having to proclaim God's word weekly and the simultaneously peculiar amusement that arises from the task.[18] In a parallel way, loving members of your church elicits a sensation of "burdensome joy." No doubt there are moments in pastoral ministry where carrying the burdens of others is toilsome. The yoke hanging around our necks can feel insufferable

17. Blanchard and Hodges, *Lead Like Jesus*, 30.
18. Massey, *Burdensome Joy of Preaching*, 13.

at worst and fatiguing at best. Pastors are often told gossip they'd rather not hear. Pastors are expected to safeguard the secrets of their parishioners as if their lives depended on it. Pastors are called on to be selfless and nurture people in various ways. Simply put, pastors die to themselves.

The sense of responsibility placed on our shoulders is unwelcome. In fact, no human being should carry all this weight on her back. For this reason, the Apostle Peter tells us to "Cast all your anxiety on him because he cares for you" (1 Pet 5:7). Pastors were never required to lay the afflictions of the world on themselves. Instead, Jesus anticipated that we would hand these burdens over to him.

When we hand parishioners' hardships over to Jesus, we can view ministry as a privilege and not a millstone. As ministers of the gospel, we are given a divine appointment to step into the broken lives of the hurting. They confide in us regarding all arenas of life and death. They share with us their marital problems, financial struggles, and their grievances with children, in-laws, and coworkers. Can you believe that our sheep deposit enough faith in us not to reveal their open sores and greatest moral lapses? If that isn't humbling, I don't know what humility is. At the same time, they count on us to celebrate with them in life's greatest festivities, such as weddings and the birth of new children. The list of obstacles and thrills is endless. Yet one thing is clear. Through good times and dire circumstances, pastors love their sheep. And there is no greater joy than being there with them through each of life's adventures.

Ask Yourself

1. Do I genuinely love my church members?

2. Am I a good listener? How can I listen more effectively?

3. How can I be more proactive in demonstrating my love for parishioners?

4. Who are the difficult people in my congregation, and how can I treat them better?

7

Expect the Unexpected

Unexpected Tragedies

Pastors hover over the front lines of the spiritual battleground. We minister to complex people living in a fallen world. Ministry can be far from tidy, and nothing can fully prepare us for what lies ahead. In this ongoing war for souls, we are not shielded by a bunker in the sand. Rather, we're exposed and completely vulnerable to all forms of attack.

Tragedy had struck my new congregation before I began my first official day. The moving truck was laden with our limited possessions: an inherited bed, a hand-me-down sofa, twenty-four boxes of books, kitchenware, and my mother-in-law's twenty-eight-year-old plant. Our new home was a driving distance of about a thousand miles away. While on the road, I noticed a missed call from one of the leaders of our new church family. On arriving at the hotel, I returned his call. The quiver in his voice indicated he was shaken up. He shared the tragic news that one of the couples in our church had lost their son in a car accident a couple days earlier. The funeral would take place the day after our arrival. I was speechless. I barely mustered up a word of condolence, and we ended the conversation.

While Jesus began his earthly ministry by attending a wedding celebration in Cana, I commenced my new life as a pastor at a funeral comforting a couple who had just lost their twenty-month-old son. This was definitely not the way I envisioned ministry beginning. But that's the reality of the pastoral office. As new pastors, we must always expect the unexpected.

During that week, the entire church came together as a unified body to pray for the couple and support them. Graciously, a local pastor oversaw the funeral arrangements. Over the years, it was my privilege to encourage these beloved members. I prayed with them and shed many tears with them. I imparted to them messages of hope from God's word. While their wounds will never be healed on this side of heaven, they took giant strides toward becoming integral members of the church family. In short, through this tragedy, they drew closer to the Lord. God can use pastors even in the most unexpected of tragedies.

This lesson describes some of these unforeseeable moments, people, and situations that enter our lives as beginning ministers. We can't prevent unexpected or uninvited situations from occurring, whether positive or negative. Derek Prime and Alistair Begg write, "No worthwhile task in any sphere is achieved without obstacles, and so they must be overcome. Unique difficulties associated with the ministry constantly beset us."[1] However, we can brace ourselves for them and depend solely on God for greater understanding and wisdom to handle all types of situations.

Unexpected Visitors

Two Sundays into my pastoral role, a family began attending our worship service. Any new and eager pastor welcomes visitors with open arms.[2] Whether they choose to plug in or move on, all churches need visitors even if it's only for the sake of congregational vitality. Gary McIntosh conveys how most congregations today will spend a significant amount of time getting ready for their company: visitors. For them it involves such things as preparing an attractive worship service, organizing teams of greeters, cleaning the church facility, offering refreshing snacks, and, most important, creating a welcoming environment.[3]

Yes, churches should embrace newcomers and make them feel welcome. Truthfully, however, I didn't want this particular family to stick around. They didn't seem to be in their right state of mind. Throughout the worship service, they kept distracting me, standing and exiting repeatedly.

1. Prime and Begg, *On Being a Pastor*, 289.

2. For resources, see Collins, *What Does it Mean to Be Welcoming?*, and Rainer, *Becoming a Welcoming Church*. I am writing a book tentatively titled *Becoming a Friendlier Church*.

3. McIntosh, *Beyond the First Visit*, 7–8.

The eyes of the woman, in particular, (who was ethnically Korean) propelled a strange demonic force. They were a bizarre shade of blue, icy and cold. I felt chills when our eyes met. In addition, their twelve-year-old son ran around the building telling the Sunday school children that he saw demons in the classrooms upstairs. Several parents were concerned about this young child and how he would influence impressionable children.

Later, we found out that this couple had been meeting with some single women in our church for several months. They came to church to find more people to influence with their brand of heretical teaching. For example, this couple told women in our congregation to leave the church immediately and to only attend their Bible studies. They were instructed, "You don't need this church to know God. Leave immediately." Moreover, the husband was obsessed with an outlandish belief that he was one of the final prophets to usher in Jesus' second coming. I suppose it was the passion and charisma of this couple that kept the women interested in their furtive meetings.

After these matters had come to the leadership's attention, some members of our church board asked this couple to discontinue meeting with members of our church and to cease attending our Sunday worship service. It wasn't that we didn't love them and care for them as lost souls. However, we needed to terminate this caustic relationship that was detrimental to members of the flock.

New ministers are bombarded with myriad concerns and thus we can all too easily get lost in our day-to-day activities and let our guards down. It's distressing to think that we can't trust every person who walks through our church's doors. However, that's the reality of the world in which we live. So at all times, be alert and shrewd when it comes to newcomers. While most visitors will be harmless, there may come a time when evil lurks nearby.

Unexpected Requests

Pastors are often asked by their parishioners to assist them in many aspects of life. Depending on the life stage of your congregation, requests will vary. For example, if your church comprises mainly university students, members of your flock may ask you to write them a recommendation for graduate school or for a potential job. They could ask you for advice on relationships or let you in on personal struggles with purity and holiness. In a congregation of mostly young adults, you might be asked to escort a couple through premarital counseling or serve as the officiant at their wedding. At a predominantly elderly church, you may even be called on to get your hands dirty and assist an elderly person to help with household chores. You may need to visit the hospital frequently or perform some funerals along the way. These are some of the usual requests that come with the territory of being a pastor. While some requests are expected, every so often you may be asked to do something out of the ordinary.

A friend of mine related how the new senior pastor of his church was asked to find a husband for a parishioner's daughter who didn't attend his church. The pastor asked this woman, "Why don't you bring her to church and maybe she'll meet a good Christian man?" To this, she replied, "Pastor, it doesn't matter whether she marries a Christian, just please find her a husband." It turns out that this family had recently immigrated to the United States and desired a green card through a swift marriage ceremony. You can never imagine what types of requests you will encounter in the ministry.

Unexpected requests will often come when we least expect them. After a worship service in which I had just preached a sermon on caring for the poor, Tony and Melissa entered the fellowship hall. Every Sunday, as a church family, we share in table fellowship over lunch. That day's menu item happened to be fried chicken. In the middle of biting into a drumstick, a congregant tapped me on the shoulder. He quietly whispered in my ear, "Tony and Melissa need some help." I gladly went over to greet them.

I could tell immediately that Tony and Melissa were in difficult circumstances. Melissa sat in her wheelchair as Tony stood hunched over behind her. They were both unkempt and wore raggedy clothing. They probably hadn't showered in days or perhaps even weeks. "How can I help you?" I asked. He replied with humble reservation:

> My name is Tony, and this is my wife Melissa. Pastor, we're not doing so well. I'm battling testicular cancer and Melissa is bound to this wheelchair. I'm in between jobs right now and we could really use some cash to visit our family in Florida. We need some money to take the Greyhound bus down there. We also could use a night's stay in a hotel to freshen up and get some sleep. Some chicken over there would be nice. If you don't mind, we'd love something to eat.

My heart broke for this couple. It was not a coincidence that they arrived on that Sunday. I felt convicted to put my sermon into action. After bringing them some food and lemonade, I called over a couple members of the leadership board. We discussed their situation and decided to lend them a hand as best as we could. We drove them to a motel nearby, paid for their night's shelter, gave them some extra money for food, and said our goodbyes.

Several months later, Tony and Melissa reemerged. On this occasion, however, the expression on Tony's countenance had changed dramatically and so had his tone of voice. Tony wasn't bashful about his request. In fact, he spoke with unashamed entitlement, saying, "Pastor, we're back and we need to stay at the La Quinta Inn. No exceptions." I didn't know what to say. From his demeanor, I had an inkling that the La Quinta Inn was of a higher quality than the motel in which they stayed the first time around. In fact, the room of their choice would cost well over $100 per night.

After our first meeting with Tony and Melissa, the church leadership decided that as the senior pastor, I would no longer deal directly with people's financial requests. It was for my safety. The leaders met with Tony. From his reaction, it was obvious that their offer was not good enough. He looked displeased and walked out the door. When I asked what happened, they replied, "Tony demanded that we put them up at the La Quinta Inn for two or three nights. End of story. When we offered a different place, he said he didn't want it."

Throughout Scripture, God communicates to us about his heart for people, especially victims of poverty, abuse, and neglect, among other hardships. In Jesus' parable of the Sheep and the Goats, he sternly commands Christians to care for the least of these by putting their faith into practice. Explicitly, he says to the goats, "For I was hungry and you gave me nothing to eat, I was thirsty and you gave me nothing to drink, I was a stranger and you did not invite me in, I needed clothes and you did not clothe me, I was sick and in prison and you did not look after me" (Matt 25:42–43).

As pastors, we need to care for the poor, the afflicted, and the marginalized. Yet the questions we raised in this situation with Tony and Melissa were: To what extent are we to help those in need? Though we must come to their aid, are we being responsible with God's resources by permitting the needy to be selective about their choice of lodging? At what point does our giving stop? I wonder how Jesus would have responded to Tony's request.

Here, in this example, we felt strongly that our offer of accommodation was sufficient and a reasonable utilization of church funds. After this incident, the church leadership decided it was necessary to write out a policy with regard to financial and other requests from members of the community. If your congregation does not already have a clear strategy in place, it may be beneficial to discuss this with your elders or leadership staff. Unfortunately, I was completely caught off guard in this scenario. Be ready for such unexpected requests. Put some guidelines in place. Know, in advance, how you will handle them. And with discernment, bestow grace and compassion on those coming to you in dire straits.

Unexpected Words

Gary Chapman, in *The Five Love Languages*, draws our attention to different ways people exchange love: (1) words of affirmation, (2) quality time, (3) receiving gifts, (4) acts of service, and (5) physical touch.[4] Based on Chapman's definition, my love language is words of affirmation. He explains, "Verbal compliments, or words of appreciation, are powerful communicators of love."[5] Ever since I was a toddler, my mom would always encourage me through her words of praise. "Matt, you can do it!" was her favorite phrase. Over the years, I have thrived on the verbal support of others. Like most, I need to hear them once in a while to keep going.

It's crucial to know yourself as a pastor, understanding not only your love languages but also your weak points. Satan will use anything he can to discourage you, especially the words of your congregants. My struggle is that I crave those elusive words of affirmation. They come less frequently than I would like, especially in the pastorate. I tend to be on the needier side. Of course, all ministers long for words that tickle our ears, such as, "Pastor, you preached a wonderful sermon today that really spoke to my heart" or "Pastor, I really appreciate all that you do for me and this congregation. Thank you very much for all of your hard work and sacrifice." As pastors, we want to feel appreciated for the earthly pleasures we often forego and the effort we put forth as full-time servants of God.

Pastoring a church where almost everyone was my senior, I often heard comments about my age. When I began my ministry there, I was twenty-nine years old. Even though it wasn't their intention to offend me, sometimes people's words stung. For instance, sometimes parishioners introduced me to others in this way: "This is Matt, our senior pastor. He doesn't look like a senior pastor, but he is." What they meant was that people might be surprised to hear that I was their senior pastor because of my youthful countenance. It was only natural that they would say this since many congregants were at least a decade older than me. When people say such things, we can emotionally

4. Chapman, *Five Love Languages*, 39–130.
5. Chapman, *Five Love Languages*, 39.

react quickly and feel disrespected or unappreciated. People don't always mean to slight you. So pastors need to grow thicker skin. It's not painless, but it will save you from heartache and consternation.

Pastoral shepherds should also brace themselves for criticism. John Vawter states, "Critics are a part of life. It's how we deal with them that makes the difference between our failure and success. . . . Pastors are called to lead. Pastors are expected to set the pace. And leaders and pacesetters are always criticized. It cannot be avoided."[6] New pastors, as difficult as it may be to turn the other cheek time after time, please be mindful that we are pastors who seek to please God first, not our parishioners. Along similar lines, Larry Kreider shares, "In an undeniable and personal way, the Lord revealed that my value comes from His love for me. And God loves me just because He loves me, not because of what I do or what people think."[7] What will enable us to struggle onward in pastoral ministry is the anticipation that God, our Father, will be satisfied with our ministry service for his kingdom. Remember, God loves us just as we are. And hopefully God will reward us with precious words of affirmation, "Well done, good and faithful servant."

Unexpected Life Situations

I had the privilege of officiating Albert and Monica's wedding ceremony. They were a beautiful couple who loved God dearly. In their first year of marriage, God blessed them with a handsome baby boy, Elijah. Albert's mother flew in from the East Coast to help them adjust to their new lives. After several months, Albert's father, George, also scheduled to pay them a visit. However, prior to his arrival date, he suddenly suffered a stroke. As a precautionary measure, he stayed home for a couple of weeks. Upon recovering to some degree, he eventually came to see his new grandson.

Days into his trip, George expressed physical discomfort. He wasn't feeling like himself. So Albert took him to the hospital. The results of his exam showed that he had a brain tumor, which most likely caused his stroke weeks earlier. Sadly, they learned that this type of tumor is one of the most aggressive forms of cancer of the brain. This prognosis was a complete shock to the entire family.

---

6. Vawter, "Handling Criticism," 143.

7. Kreider, *Authentic Spiritual Mentoring*, 86. See also Im, *You Are What You Do.*

One Sunday, after the worship service, Albert informed me that since his arrival, George had grown as a Christian. For the better part of his life, he was a skeptic. Yet through God's providence and mercy, George accepted Jesus Christ as his personal Lord and Savior, and he wanted to be baptized. Albert asked me if I would perform George's baptism. I was honored to share in heaven's celebration.

The next day Sarah and I went to Albert's home. We shared a meal. Later that evening, I asked George a few questions regarding his conversion experience and then I baptized George. It was a powerful moment. Someone who was so close to death had now experienced new life in Jesus Christ, and he wanted to profess his faith to others. Ten days later, George breathed his last. And I was given the special opportunity to speak a message of hope into the lives of a small group of family and friends during the graveside service.

Unexpected life situations like these are unpredictable in the course of one's ministry. As pastors, we have been presented with an opportunity to share in the aspects of parishioners' lives to which others simply do not have access. Although I was performing a baptism and later burying the deceased, I was the one who was being blessed in the process. Words cannot express that type of joy and privilege as a minister of the gospel. All praise and glory be to God.

Unexpected Blessings

Not all unexpected matters are off-putting in pastoral ministry. Sometimes God gives us a taste of the fruit that we are bearing in and through our people. These rays of hope are what I call unexpected blessings.

Preaching is difficult work, and I spent lots of time in sermon preparation. For a pastor, proclaiming God's word faithfully is a primary goal. On behalf of the congregation, one of my aims in preaching was for God to transform lives. I wanted God to do something supernatural in the lives of my people every week. Ronald Allen writes, "Preaching can lead the community to identify ways in which we can be in partnership with God to pursue the divine intentions."[8] When our preaching seems unsuccessful at engendering change, it can feel depleting.

As I began my preaching ministry at the church, due to my need for affirmation, I naïvely formed opinions about what people thought of

8. Allen, *Preaching and Practical Ministry*, 43.

my sermons based on their posture or facial expressions. Every so often, I looked up and there would be people either nodding off or even rolling their eyes at what God was communicating through me. During the first few months, my wife began a prayer ministry with several women at the church. Every Wednesday, a handful of women would gather to share prayer requests and intercede for each other and the congregation. Oftentimes the meetings would last several hours. We also launched a Saturday morning prayer meeting. In due course, there were hardly any congregants sleeping in the pews and people stopped rolling their eyes. What a testimony to God's ability to change hearts.

When I first went to that church, no meetings took place outside of the Sunday worship service. There were no Bible studies, no small group meetings, no Wednesday or Friday night fellowship, zero outreach activities, absolutely nothing. The leadership of the church decided that the best way to get members plugged in was through small groups. At first, I didn't want to lead my own small group on top of everything else that I was doing. I thought that I could just train others to lead small groups, because I could then use my time in other ways to benefit the church. My wife convinced me otherwise. I'm so glad that she did.

During our small group leaders training, we partitioned the church membership roster into twelve small groups: men's groups, women's groups, and couple's groups. We placed every single person into a group. As time went on, I noticed that everyone assigned to my group was a fringe member of the congregation. The one commonality among these participants was a passion for sports. We were known affectionately as the jock group. Every week, we convened at the church for dinner and had a brief discussion about a chapter from a Christian book on men's issues. At the outset, people didn't seem comfortable. Perhaps meeting at the church building was threatening.

My wife came up with the brilliant idea to have the group meet in our home instead. This made a noticeable difference. Over time, this group of guys who were once erratic in their church attendance became committed to both small groups and attending the Sunday service. They gradually shared intimate details about their personal lives. They increasingly participated in more church activities. We served the homeless together by cooking a meal for families in need. In short, we made significant progress from those early meetings. My small group members gave me life and hope in so many ways. They became an unexpected source of joy and encouragement in the ministry. When we left the church six years later, nearly everyone was involved in a small group.

When he so chooses, God pours out his favor upon pastors with unexpected blessings. The stories above are a mere glimpse into numerous ways that I saw God at work in the congregation. I can't count the number of ways God changed people in the church and matured them in their faith. These unforeseen miracles compel us to persevere through tough seasons in pastoral ministry. They remind us that we're not in control, but God is. And God's grace is enough for us.

Ask Yourself

1. What fears do I have as I enter the pastorate?

2. Where am I vulnerable in areas of temptation? How will I guard against falling into sin?

3. How will I respond to unexpected tragedies, visitors, requests, comments, life situations, and blessings? Does my church have strategies in place to handle them?

4. To whom will I turn for guidance and help in rough situations?

Conclusion

What is a Successful Pastor?

A TREND IN AMERICAN evangelicalism is to determine the worth of a pastor by what is quantifiable, such as Sunday worship attendance, the size of the church's membership, the annual budget, or the number of programs. The media seems to value only the opinions of pastors leading large congregations, which indirectly communicates to the pastors of smaller churches that we have nothing worthwhile to say. Church buildings resemble flashy sporting arenas more than they do worship-filled sanctuaries. For the pastor of a small church in North America, it can be rather defeating to witness others' achievements in comparison to our church's perceived mediocrity or stagnancy.

It's difficult not to envy those who appear to be doing everything right. A question that begs our attention is, what defines a successful ministry and pastorate? For some of us, how we define success will impact our longevity in a specific church. It will enable us to see past the numbers. Without hesitation, I can tell you plainly that only God can judge whether or not we have been successful shepherds. As this book comes to an end, I hope that you will desire faithfulness more than fruitfulness in the pastorate.

The Search for Significance

Every person wants to be significant and leave an indelible mark on this world. Jeffrey Miller writes, "Often men spend the first half of their professional life comparing themselves to others and pursuing success. We spend the second half pursuing significance."[1] What does significance mean to the average pastor? Robert McGee in *The Search for Significance* provides the world's formula for success: "Self-Worth = Performance (what you do) + Others' Opinions (what others think or say about you)."[2]

This equation is the cultural norm, but it's not necessarily on par with God's standards. In this world, our relentless pursuit to become somebody in this life usually falls on deaf ears. Ultimately nobody cares about our accomplishments on this earth. The more we succeed according to the world's standards, the more people will dislike us or envy our achievements. God's paradigm for success usually contradicts what our parishioners deem astonishing or sensational. Contrasting the ways of the world, McGee offers God's equation for success: "Self-Worth = God's Truth about You."[3]

Most of us will start out our ministry journey in a conventional way after completing our seminary training and serve as children's pastors, youth pastors, college ministry pastors, worship pastors, or some type of assistant/associate pastors. Some will be called to the senior pastorate of a smaller congregation. Yet in God's perspective, there is no ministerial hierarchy. Sadly, we in the church have created an imaginary ministry ladder. As in a business corporation, young pastors feel like they must begin as a children's pastor or a youth pastor, but the ultimate objective is to become the senior pastor of a large, well-known church. I don't think that's how God envisions his blueprint for ministry.

But pastors are human, too. Many are type A personalities with great ambition. Recently, when I asked my students in pastoral ministry class if they secretly wanted to become "a successful, well-known pastor" everyone put their eyes down. I had my answer. While there's nothing wrong with being a goal-oriented person, Jody Seymour rightly asserts, "Clergypersons would be healthier if we faced up to our ambition, named it, and claimed it. Knowing what confession means, it would be appropriate to admit our jealousy of one another. Perhaps if we confessed our personal ambitions and envy, we could go on to some renewal of a true covenant community relationship."[4] The key to a successful ministry is trusting that God knows us better than we know ourselves. God is the one who created

1. Miller, *Hazards of Being a Man*, 163.
2. McGee, *Search for Significance*, 160.
3. McGee, *Search for Significance*, 160.
4. Seymour, *Time for Healing*, 10.

us. God knows what we can and cannot handle. God knows our gifts and our Achilles' heels. That's why God has placed us in a particular ministry context for a reason. To be successful and significant is serving God passionately and faithfully with our entire heart, body, mind, and soul in the place to which he's called us.

We Can't Please Everyone

Along the same lines, all humans want to be liked. Again, pastors are no exception. We want to be liked by our parishioners and other local ministers, as well as members of our denominations and communities. But there will always be those in our parish that will be disappointed with us. We simply can't please everyone. Frank Minirth and his colleagues attest to the reality that "the pastor who is liked by everyone doesn't exist. No matter who you are and how hard you try, you are not going to be universally loved and accepted and neither is your family."[5]

Soong-Chan Rah helps us see that our function as pastors transcends meeting individualized felt needs and concerns of our parishioners:

> On Monday mornings, I often picture the faces of individual members who were disappointed that I did not speak to their specific need for that week. I am also aware that even if I make every effort to meet every personal and individual need, someone will still not have had his or her personal needs met. Maybe a larger and more important question is: why am I trying so hard to meet the specific and personal needs of the individual?[6]

Trying to please the masses is a universal trap for pastors. We yearn to see the smiles of doting church members instead of the jeering frowns of those we have upset. With each desperate go at satisfying different pockets of people and certain individuals, we fail to please God. We become enslaved to what people think of us rather than what God thinks of us. Our sense of worth is corroborated not by the creator of the universe but by his creations. Eventually, we become so imprisoned to a life of people pleasing that the shackles feel unbreakable. People pleasing may kill our ministry effectiveness.

5. Minirth et al., *What They Didn't Teach*, 20–21.
6. Rah, *Next Evangelicalism*, 28.

Regardless of our calling as pastors, we should live in a way that pleases God alone. Jesus once asked the provocative question in Luke 9:25, "What good is it for someone to gain the whole world, and yet lose or forfeit their very self?" Likewise, I ask pastors, "How does it profit us if we gain the approval of humans but forfeit the applause of God who matters most?" My prayer is that this next generation of pastors will live and serve with an eternal perspective. We can't expect or demand instant gratification from God. Make your decisions based on God's values and God's plans, for he will be the one that judges our every thought and deed.

Bigger Does Not Mean Better

As North Americans, we often value quantity over quality. In other words, we've bought into the philosophy that bigger means better. For instance, when we were living in the United Kingdom, we would frequent the local grocery store almost every day. By contrast, North Americans sometimes own two refrigerators so that we can make just one stop at a warehouse club to purchase all the family's food and household needs for weeks.[7] In doing so, we have convinced ourselves that mass equals value.

Somehow, this same philosophy has permeated our churches. Will God reward pastors of bigger churches more than pastors of smaller ones? Let's learn a simple but profound lesson from Jesus' parable of the Talents. As his disciples question him about the signs of the last days, Jesus shares a parable with his disciples. This time it concerns a master who goes away on a trip. He entrusts property to his three servants. One receives five talents, another servant acquires two talents, while the third is given one talent.

Each servant is expected to build on the master's wealth. The master anticipates a positive return from his servants. The first two servants who receive five and two talents, respectively, double their money. They were shrewd and diligent investors. On his return, the master calls them to account, and he's equally pleased with their results. The master's response to both servants is indistinguishable: "His master replied, 'Well done, good and faithful servant! You have been faithful with a few things; I will put you in charge of many things. Come and share your master's happiness!'" (Matt 25:21, 23). This third servant, however, found excuses for his inability to yield a profit. He dug a hole in the ground and later returned the talent

---

7. Yes, the COVID-19 pandemic has pushed us to shop in mass quantities.

to his master. If he had simply done what the others did, he would have received the same praise from his lord.

One day God will call each of us to account for the talents he's freely given. What God desires is that we make the most use of those talents. God never expects that a person receiving one talent will gain five more. Yet God wants us to invest properly so that we receive a positive return. In the church context, that means being faithful to God by using the gifts God has given us to make disciples and expand his kingdom.

God is Faithful

The Apostle Paul writes the following to the Christians at Corinth: "He will also keep you firm to the end, so that you will be blameless on the day of our Lord Jesus Christ. God is faithful, who has called you into fellowship with his Son, Jesus Christ our Lord" (1 Cor 1:8–9). Pastoral ministry is not about the fruit that we bear or what we can accomplish by human determination. We are simply powerless to change people.

The wonderful truth about pastoral ministry is that we are only called to plant the seeds, but God is the one who makes those seeds grow. Since God is faithful, he cares more about our faithfulness than our fruitfulness. The authors of *What They Didn't Teach You in Seminary* remind us:

> Pastors, please let us encourage you in the concept of being faithful. Different churches are at different stages of their lives. For some, it is a time to sow; for others it is a time to nurture. For still others, it is a time to reap. Too many churches measure their church against another church, their pastor against another pastor. It isn't fair. Any minister should only be measured against his own potential, the circumstances of the area in which his ministry is located, and his faithfulness to God. To do the best you can is to be successful.[8]

Churches need pastors who will not only ride the high tides of fertile ministry but stick it out—especially in dry, sometimes fruitless spiritual times. The people sitting in the pews are yearning to see ministers who won't quit on them at the first signs of conflict. The world is waiting to see pastors who are so passionate about their calling that they are willing to abandon personal aspirations, bigger salaries, and individual accolades. As Rick Reed puts it simply, "Besides, we went into ministry to be faithful, not

8. Minirth et al., *What They Didn't Teach*, 229.

famous."[9] God's people require pastors who are committed wholeheartedly to teaching right doctrine. We need pastors who will not cave into the pressures of pleasing people and affirming the philosophies and paradigms of an unbelieving and hostile society. In short, the church of God is longing for humble, faithful shepherds.

This book has hopefully given you a glimpse into the joys and challenges of pastoral ministry. In it, I've openly exposed my experiences in the first year of the pastorate. I had many ups and downs, and yet I continue to live and serve with great hope in the one who called me. While every church is unique, our role as pastoral shepherds is clear and simple. We are called to love God and to love the people we serve. We represent Jesus to a broken and hurting world that needs the message of God's love revealed in the person and work of Christ.

Derek Prime and Alistair Begg write, "Success in spiritual work is not synonymous with being in the public eye or even being regarded by God's people as successful. Success is finishing the work God has given us, and no one else, to do."[10] No doubt, ministry can be extremely challenging. The church we are called to serve isn't perfect, but remember we're not perfect either. And yet in God's providence, God has placed you there for a specific reason. As you submit to God's will, please keep in mind that God "is able to do immeasurably more than all we ask or imagine, according to his power that is at work within us" (Eph 3:20). But, notice what the next verse says, "to him be glory in the church and in Christ Jesus throughout all generations, for ever and ever! Amen" (Eph 3:21). As we persevere in the ministry, God will receive the glory for our invaluable labor. While your sufferings for Christ are real, your efforts are not in vain. I pray that these seven lessons will guide you in the first year of the pastorate and beyond; and I'm hopeful that you will be faithful to God in the exciting journey ahead.

Ask Yourself

1. How do I define success as a pastor?

2. How has this book changed my perception of pastoral ministry?

3. What additional questions did it raise as I begin my pastorate?

4. What is my ultimate goal in being a minister of the gospel?

9. Reed, *Heart of the Preacher*, 28.
10. Prime and Begg, *On Being a Pastor*, 307.

7.1

Cultivate Your Character

Pastoral Temptations

NOBODY ENTERS MINISTRY PLANNING to commit moral failure of any kind. On his blog, Carey Nieuwhof writes, "They didn't begin in leadership by hoping 'one day I hope I have an affair/steal money/destroy my family/ruin my church/disillusion many/lose my soul.'"[1] Moral failure can happen to anyone, however, when we become lax about our Christian character. One sinful thought can lead us astray. This first bonus lesson urges us to cultivate our character.

While there are numerous definitions of character, Scott M. Gibson says, "Character is a God-shaped self-discipline that acts with consistency."[2] As the media continues to remind us, pastors are often susceptible to lapses in judgment, particularly in the areas of finances and sexual purity. Whether you are a pastor in a large metropolis, an affluent suburb, or a rural context, all kinds of temptations abound. Some are more susceptible to temptation with regard to sexual immorality, power, envy, greed, abuse of authority, gossip, or any other sin issue. Terry Linhart suggests five common areas of potential weakness among pastors in *The Self-Aware Leader*: seeking prominence, holding on to control, valuing shiny stuff, pursuing inappropriate intimacy, and relishing resentment.[3] In this section, I'll ad-

1. Nieuwhof, "5 Reasons Pastors Fail Morally."
2. Gibson, "Preacher's Character," 14.
3. Linhart, *Self-Aware Leader*, 77–96.

dress shiny stuff and inappropriate intimacy (à la Linhart), and then move on to some other character issues.

First, regarding the potential for financial impropriety, Curtis Thomas observes how pastoral integrity can become suspect when we have personal access to the church's capital. He states, "One of the quickest ways for a pastor to raise needless questions about his integrity, to become burdened with things unnecessary, and to be tempted to treat members with partiality is to become involved in the church's finances."[4] We have seen over the years how money has corrupted many influential pastors.

Our church's finance administrator was out of town for a weekend. At the end of the service, one parishioner who assists in counting the tithes and offerings didn't know what to do since this financial process was normally shared by at least two individuals. He gave me the bag of offering and asked, "Would you mind holding on to this for a week, and we'll calculate the total next Sunday?" Thomas admonishes that pastors may have a say in how the church's resources are employed to some extent; however, cash or checks shouldn't touch our hands.[5] My mind raced at that moment. It felt like a strange scene from a movie with blaring audio effects—duh, duh, duh—the pastor holding the offering bag. What do I do now? If I took the tithes and offerings home, there was always room for speculation that I embezzled funds. It would also be tempting for me to see how much money individual members contributed. I didn't want to know how much people gave to the Lord. Immediately, I gave these monetary gifts to one of our steering committee members so that he and another leader could take care of the situation. I didn't want to be involved.

Be circumspect with regard to how you deal with money issues. Congregants are always aware of what we do. So honor God with your finances. Even though our salaries may be lower than the average parishioner's, be an example in the areas of tithing and giving. If we preach on sacrificial giving but do not practice it, we will be found out, and our witness will be undermined. Also, be mindful of how you choose to spend God's resources whether that is your personal salary or the church's budget. Err on the side of giving to others rather than desiring more for yourself and your family. Trust that God promises to take care of his children.

Another strong force of temptation for pastors concerns sexual impropriety in all its forms. Shortly after beginning at a ministry, a scandal

---

4. Thomas, *Practical Wisdom for Pastors*, 108.
5. Thomas, *Practical Wisdom for Pastors*, 108.

broke out in a congregation close by. The youth minister, who was a single male, had carried on an inappropriate sexual relationship with a young teenaged girl in his youth group. Admitting his guilt publicly, he was later charged with sexual assault on a child. No doubt this exploitation devastated that church.

No pastor is immune from sexual sin. Single ministers are equally as vulnerable as married ones. Bill Perkins writes in *When Good Men Are Tempted*, "Yet even though we're new men in Christ, we still must deal with the lustful appetites that reside within us. These have not been taken away or changed. But they do not define who we are."[6] Let's face it: The message of sex is all around us. Engaging in premarital sex and having sex with someone other than your spouse are glorified acts in today's society. The media promotes everyone to have more sexual partners and sexual experiences.

Pastors are falling into sexual sin at rapid rates. For example, pornography use among pastors continues to soar. Barna found that "most pastors (57%) and youth pastors (64%) admit they have struggled with porn, either currently or in the past . . . 55% of pastors who use porn say they live in constant fear of being discovered."[7] What about the pastors who are unwilling to report their sins? The secret cycle of sexual sin can begin anywhere, at any time and with anyone. We may not even suspect the path of ruin in which we are traveling. Before we know it, we can tear God's covenant of marriage, divide the family unit, wreck churches, fracture the faith of our parishioners, and keep polluting the image of Christian ministers in a skeptical world.

As in the case of the aforementioned youth minister, sexual sin in the pastorate can commence when counseling members of the opposite sex for multiple counseling sessions or spending time alone with someone to whom we are attracted.[8] Kenneth Swetland describes a case study of one such pastor, Pete, who acted upon his sexual feelings for a married congregant. After counseling her for a period of time, a strong intimacy developed between them. Swetland recounts the following:

> Don and Janie invited Pete and Barbara over for dinner a few days after settling into their new home. Pete sensed that he shouldn't go because the thought of seeing Janie was too exciting. Pete often hugged his parishioners and would kiss women on the

6. Perkins, *When Good Men Are Tempted*, 11.
7. See Kinnaman, "The Porn Phenomenon."
8. Swetland, *Hidden World of the Pastor*, 27.

cheek (many parishioners had commented on how warm and affectionate he was), but as he and Janie embraced at the door of their home he felt more was being communicated than socially accepted affection. Again he was frightened by his feelings, but he felt helpless to control them.[9]

In the end, Pete committed adultery, divorced his wife Barbara, and married Janie, who in this ordeal also divorced Don.

However, we must not seal shut the idea of ministry to both genders. It is possible, permissible, and sometimes necessary to minister to someone of the opposite gender. Every member is a member of the body of Christ, whether male or female, and needs to grow in Christlikeness. But we must also remember that everyone, including ourselves, is susceptible to temptation and succumbing to our sinful nature. We must be truthful to ourselves: Why are we meeting with this person? Is there something more than Christian discipleship that we secretly desire? Is it best for someone else to disciple them or work with them? The confusing part is that even while we can know ourselves and guard our thoughts, we can also deceive ourselves. We can convince ourselves that we won't fall into temptation.[10] That happens to others, not to me. Be careful as moral failure can happen to any of us.

In general, men and women should be able to work together for the sake of Christ. As Tish Harrison Warren comments, "People need meaningful relationships with members of the opposite sex, and they need them to be safe, honoring, and full of integrity."[11] In her article, "It's Not Billy Graham Rule or Bust," she offers several best practices for her and her husband (who is also a pastor) to "not only guard against adultery but to build intimacy and trust in our marriage."[12] Depending on the situation, we can minister to, disciple, and work with someone of the opposite gender, but with appropriate safeguards in place and with discretion and accountability. This interaction must never be kept private. Make it public knowledge to your spouse (if married), to your church leadership, and meet in public spaces. Perhaps the best way to disciple or work with the opposite gender is through one-on-two or one-on-three mentor-mentee relationships. If you find yourself attracted to someone other than your spouse or someone is interested in you (for those

---

9. Swetland, *Hidden World of the Pastor*, 27.

10. See Everhart, *#MeToo Reckoning*, and DeMuth, *We Too*.

11. Warren, "It's Not Billy Graham Rule or Bust."

12. Warren, "It's Not Billy Graham Rule or Bust."

who are married), heed Joseph's example and flee from temptation. Don't flirt with temptation, run away (Gen 39:10).

New pastors, please pray that God would keep your hearts and minds pure. We must pray for wholeness in our marital relationships. Find and maintain accountability. We can sign up for accountability services such as Covenant Eyes, which monitors our screen use and sends regular reports to the people who keep us accountable.[13] Immediately tell trusted friends if any form of attraction emerges with a member of your congregation or elsewhere, or if you find yourself searching for pornography or dwelling on other sexual sins.

Other Character Issues

Beyond money and sex, other character issues may come to the surface. Character formation is a constant battle for all believers, including ministers of the gospel. Aaron Menikoff explains in *Character Matters*, "None of us has arrived at our final destination. . . . Unfortunately, pastors can lead their congregations to think their own fight against sin is already over."[14] It is a constant battle to conform our way of thinking and living into the image of Christ (Rom 12:1–2).

Over the years, I have witnessed many students come and go at the seminary. Some have been blessed with numerous pastoral gifts equally matched with a humble, God-honoring spirit. There have been others, however, to whom I wish I could've graciously but directly advised: "You shouldn't go into pastoral ministry. Your pride and unteachable spirit will wound a lot of people." It's unfortunate but you've come across people and pastors like this in your lives as well. You wonder, "How did someone like *you* end up in ministry?"

For seminarians and pastors, any sin can attack us especially when we are tired, discouraged, and vulnerable. Sometimes these sins are more subtle. Here are some questions to consider: Are we engaging in behaviors (addictive or otherwise) that we justify as being a minor vice? How is our thought life? How is our prayer life? Are we lax on spending time with the Lord? Are we closed off to correction or constructive criticism? Do we ever admit that we are wrong? Do we get defensive easily? Do we confess our sin to others and seek forgiveness? Do we compare ourselves to others? Are we

13. Register for Covenant Eyes at www.covenanteyes.com.
14. Menikoff, *Character Matters*, 19.

becoming narcissistic? Do we lack empathy for others? Are we willing to serve others and listen to them? Will we do ministry service when nobody sees us, acknowledges us, or gives us the credit?

Moral lapses can occur in essentially any area of life. Scott M. Gibson notes, "Larceny, sex-abuse, assault, homosexuality, plagiarism, and other offenses make the headlines about wayward preachers."[15] In theological institutions, Gibson adds, "Classes have become substitutes for discipleship and grades replaced the markers of maturity and character."[16] Rather, Gibson encourages pastors to pursue various markers of Christian maturity in Scripture such as the Sermon on the Mount (Matt 5–7), the Fruit of the Spirit (Gal 5:22–23), the Qualifications of an Elder (1 Tim 3:2–7 and Titus 2:6–9), Elders and the Flock (1 Pet 5:1–11), and like passages.[17]

Take some time to wrestle with the heart issues in these passages. How are we doing in each of these areas of character formation and discipleship? What prematurely ends a pastorate, as we know, is not typically one's preaching, teaching, counseling, or pastoral care, but rather the pastor's lack of character. I would listen to a preacher who has a little less competence but who's not deficient in character. I would not, however, listen to a preacher who is deficient in character but had a little more competence. As Bob Burg and John David Mann share in *The Go-Giver Leader*, "Competence matters. Character matters more."[18]

Conclusion

I titled this chapter using the word *cultivate* intentionally. Another way to say cultivate is "to till," such as tilling the soil. When we leave soil alone, moss covers the surface and weeds lurk above and below. It's unusable. If I could, I would show you a picture of my backyard as Example A. But when we till or cultivate the surface, we are able to "prepare and use [the ground] for the raising of crops."[19] The soil can only be useful after it's been cultivated. In a similar way, we can only be useful for ministry when we continue to regularly cultivate and till our minds and hearts and remove

---

15. Gibson, "Landscape of the Character of Preaching," 21.

16. Gibson, "Landscape of the Character of Preaching," 30.

17. Gibson, "Character of Preaching," class notes.

18. Burg and Mann, *Go-Giver Leader*, 147.

19. See https://www.merriam-webster.com/dictionary/cultivate.

the moss and weeds also known as sins. Ask your church members to commit to praying for you and your family every day.[20]

I'm a sinner saved by grace, just like you. So I share this lesson not because I think I'm somehow more Christlike, disciplined, or obedient. There are myriad sins that I struggle with daily, just as you do. But as your fellow teammate I want to remind us that through Christ we have already won the eternal championship game. Let's cultivate our character each day so that in the words of Daniel Henderson we might experience a "glorious finish."[21]

Don't listen to the whispers of the enemy. You can't just give into sin and expect restoration, to plant a new church or continue in ministry leadership.[22] No sin is ever worth forfeiting your family or your ministry. Be ruthless over your sins. Confess them regularly to trusted friends. Tear these sins out of your life. To be able to serve Christ to the end, we must cultivate our character by giving others permission to "teach, rebuke, correct and train [us] in righteousness" (2 Tim 3:16). As you pursue humility and vulnerability, allow others to speak into your life so that God can prepare the soil (our mind and heart) for kingdom work day by day, week by week, and year after year.[23]

20. See Byun, *Praying for Your Pastor.*
21. Henderson, *Glorious Finish.*
22. Shellnutt, "Beyond Cedarville."
23. See Smith, *Vulnerable Pastor.*

7.2

Practice Your Pastoral Skills

An Age of "Expertise"

WE ARE LIVING IN an age when increasingly everyone thinks they are experts. We might call it the "age of entitlement," "the age of self-absorption," or "the age of narcissism." Yet giving an opinion is not the same as pronouncing expertise. We feel entitled to many things in life from possessions to promotions to even the incessant praise of others. Ask yourself: how do I feel when I post something on social media and get very little or no attention for it?

I'm reminded of the countless singing auditions over the years for *American Idol* (yes, I confess that I watch it), where tone-deaf contestants actually believe they are phenomenal singers. Similarly, it can be hard to admit that perhaps we're not so gifted or prepared for ministry as we think we are. We could use some constructive criticism. I hate to sound so blunt, but over the years, I have witnessed a number of seminarians who need a lot of practice and words of constructive criticism. Nobody wants to hear such news about ourselves. But everyone needs it, including and especially me.

Since the earliest times in Egypt and Babylon (eighteenth century BC), every worthwhile trade had an apprenticeship where an apprentice would learn under the tutelage of his or her artisan the necessary skills for one's craft.[1] In our more recent history, apprentice artists, carpenters, cobblers, ironworkers, printers, and even professional vocations like physicians and

---

1. *Encyclopedia Britannica*, "Apprenticeship."

lawyers would receive extensive training with hands-on skills acquired through trial by fire. As we know from the Gospels, apprenticeship was also Jesus' philosophy of life and ministry. He began working from a young age as a carpenter/mason receiving mentoring on how to be skilled at his vocation. Later, in his earthly ministry, Jesus had twelve apprentices who learned what it meant to be his disciple through 24/7 monitoring and mentoring. Jesus lent them his watchful eye as he evaluated their skills for ministry and offered sage wisdom on how to do it more effectively.

Yet, sadly, for many pastors today (seminarians, pastoral interns, as well as beginning and experienced pastors), pastoral skills are learned on the fly, on site, with little or no preparation, supervision, correction, or encouragement. But, here's the problem: many still think they're doing great. Some congregants may be scared to say it: they want and need us to practice our pastoral skills.

Be an Apprentice and Make an Apprentice

Pastors and seminarians today need mentors. Just as professional athletes have a coach or mentor, everyone needs a mentor. Pastoring is not all that different from other professions or crafts. Pastors need advice and practical coaching on how to improve their ministry skills and have working knowledge prior to being thrown into the actual ministry event or moment. For instance, how does one lead a worship service, pray publicly, conduct weddings and funerals, lead a church business meeting, counsel congregants, talk to people, deal with church conflict, do pastoral visitation, and other significant ministry matters?

Having pastoral experience for a decade in various capacities (i.e., youth pastor, college pastor, and senior pastor), a decade of teaching experience at the seminary level as a professor of preaching and ministry, and also serving as the Director of the Haddon W. Robinson Center for Preaching and Director of Mentored Ministry at Gordon-Conwell Theological Seminary, I have worshiped in many churches and have witnessed scores of pastors in ministerial action. While many are competent pastors, we could all use some tips and reminders for improving our pastoral skills, especially those beginning the pastoral journey.

This final bonus lesson offers considerations for practicing pastoral skills without being overly prescriptive and denominationally specific. You may refer to it prior to the moment when your ministry skills are put to the test or maybe even after you remembered that they were discussed here in these pages. My hope is that you won't go into pastoral ministry uninformed. Let me first serve as a ministry mentor and provide you with some initial practical advice for which pastoral skills to work on. Next, I want to encourage you to find mentor(s) in ministry and make apprentice(s) as well. Find someone you trust who's skilled in the areas of ministry that you want to grow in and get their "feedforward" and feedback. Do the same for someone else.

Pastoral Skills Worth Practicing

Business Skills

We discussed the general topic of developing our leadership in chapter 5. While pastoral ministry is not a business by any means, there are skills in business that require familiarity even as a gospel minister. Two areas in church ministry that involve business leadership and acumen include: leading a church business meeting and creating/overseeing the church's budget and by-laws. Since many seminarians are recent college graduates without much business experience, it's critical to learn about these essential aspects of pastoral leadership.

The church business meeting, depending on the denomination and/ or traditions, may be formal or informal. If it is formal, we will want to become familiar with *Robert's Rules of Order,* which is a guide for parliamentary procedure. Sounds pretentious, doesn't it? Why do I need to learn about that, you may ask? These "rules" encourage orderly conduct within a business or organization and govern how decisions are made collectively. Now in its twelfth edition, *Robert's Rules* is commonly employed in various denominations such as the Presbyterian Church in America.[2] Entering a pastorate that employs *Robert's Rules* will necessitate that we understand general and specific principles. If your congregation does not have a formal system as such in place, you will still want to ask prior to the first session/ elder/deacon meeting about how meetings are conducted.

In addition to church business meetings, you will want to learn about budgets and by-laws. The church budget obviously is more complex than a family's budget (if you are disciplined to have one). The church's budget will include not only pastoral and staff salaries, health insurance, and other

2. See Robert III et al., *Robert's Rules of Order.*

benefits, it will also be used to allocate funds for the work of the ministry, local and global. There are helpful resources out there for planning and creating a God-honoring church budget.[3] You will want to prayerfully consider with your leadership and congregation how best to steward God's resources short-term and long-term. The church by-laws are another necessary document that you'll want to read and get to know well. The by-laws act as a handbook and legal document in the event that things go badly and disciplinary measures are needed. During the first year, familiarize yourself with the church's method of conducting leadership meetings as well as the budget and by-laws. Many of us are not naturally gifted in leading meetings. So it may sound silly or superfluous, but you may want to practice and walk through a church business meeting with family, friends, or a small group.

Cultural Exegesis Skills

In our increasingly diverse world, another significant arena of ministry development concerns cultural exegesis skills.[4] Just as we are trained in biblical exegesis, the cultural exegete puts into practice what they've learned about the wider culture and congregational demographics. These are important as we undertake ministry relationships, counseling, evangelism, discipleship, service, preaching, and teaching in a diverse congregation. This diversity manifests itself in terms of race, ethnicity, socio-economics, education, denomination, theology, politics, sexual orientation, spiritual levels, and more. Even in what appears to be a homogeneous church setting, there are numerous forms of diversity or "subcultures."[5]

Where does one start? Get to know the demographics of your church and the surrounding neighborhoods. Is your state, politically speaking, a blue state or red state? How about your congregation members? One of easiest ways to learn about the cultural identities and perspectives in your church will be to send out an anonymous survey in the first few months. Keith Willhite, in his book *Preaching with Relevance*, provides numerous helpful categories of the types of information you'll want to seek as a new pastor in your church.[6] There is no better way to learn about the people in

---

3. See Hillman, Jr. and Reece, *Smart Church Finances*, and Dunlop, *Budgeting for a Healthy Church*.

4. For assistance on cultural exegesis, see my *Preaching with Cultural Intelligence*.

5. Tisdale, *Preaching as Local Theology*, xi.

6. Willhite, *Preaching with Relevance*, ch. 1.

your church than to meet regularly with your parishioners. Although you'll naturally gravitate towards people like yourself, make concerted efforts to spend time with people who look differently, think differently, and even act differently. Cultural exegesis is something that we can improve upon as we make it more of a natural part of who we are. As we get to know our congregants, it will become less uncomfortable as we forge relationships in the church with culturally diverse members.

Social Skills

A third area of practice concerns social skills. While it sounds obvious, social skills are often lacking among pastors—especially introverted ones. In the medical field they call it "bedside manner," while others call it having "people skills." I raise this issue because there are many pastors and pastors-in-training who simply lack social awareness and social courtesies. For instance, as I interact with students at a theological seminary, I can't tell you how many students are not able to say hello to me as I walk by them. Even as I smile and extend a greeting, they avoid eye contact altogether and stare at the pavement in front of them.

In chapter 7, we established that "ministry is people." To minister effectively, we need to be able to listen to and talk to people. As an introvert, I have known the pain of "having to talk to people." If you're anything like me, my idea of a nightmare is entering a room, for a social gathering or otherwise, where I don't know anyone. I can't think of many situations in life that are worse for an introvert. And yet, we pastor people and not books and ideas. The entire purpose of pastoral study is to communicate to and relate to God's people. That means we need to work on our social skills. Again, it may sound like I'm stretching it too far. But I'm not. Practice smiling at people, waving to them, and greeting them. Practice having a conversation with someone who is not your family member. As much as it pains you, learn and even force yourself to engage in small talk and long talk. People skills require practice. Keep doing it every chance you get.

Worship Skills

Finally, it's critical that we practice skills in leading worship. I'm not referring to the singing or praise portion of the worship service per se, although our vocal cords may require exercise as well if that's our pastoral responsibility. No, I'm specifically referring here to elements of the worship service that are public and in front of people. That would include some of the following: the call to worship, the prayer of invocation, responsive reading, liturgies, recitation of creeds, pastoral prayer, announcements, Scripture reading, the sermon, and the benediction.[7]

I'm sure you can appreciate this imaginary, embarrassing worship service moment. You or someone comes up to read the Scripture for the impending sermon. You or this person has decided not to rehearse reading the Scripture passage. "How hard could it be," we quip to ourselves? It's just reading! Later, our stomachs churn as we mumble and fumble our way through the text as our faces glow amber red and sweat trickles down our cheeks. We didn't realize that this passage included the dreaded names of Hebrew characters. We slightly botch or grossly mispronounce almost every single name. When will this thing end? Even when names are not involved, Scripture reading and many other parts of the worship service mentioned above can be done poorly and off-puttingly. Have you slipped up yourself or witnessed such a humbling scene? It doesn't have to be that way.

Conclusion

God deserves our best. For this reason, we must practice, practice, and practice some more. It's not enough to have it written out and in front of us. Ink on paper is not the same as practicing beforehand. We must actually say the words out loud and hear them with our own ears. Listen to your voice, your tone, your demeanor. I would argue even for practicing the announcements. How many awkwardly done announcement moments can you count? Probably too many. We want to give the Lord our best in worship. Practice every aspect of the worship service out loud. Train your worship participants and leaders to do the same.

In this final lesson, I want to remind us of the importance of practicing our pastoral skills. Whether it's leading a business meeting, exegeting the culture, social skills or worship skills, find ways to practice. Each week figure out what responsibilities you have and then practice them. Go over the business meeting agenda, the sermon, the responsive reading, the benediction, and every other public communication and say them out loud at least once or twice. Hear yourself pronouncing words, phrases, punctuation, and more. Don't rely on mere gifts, abilities, and "I know what I'm doing and I've done that before" self-talk. Practice all of your pastoral skills.

7. Useful resources include Currie, *Big Idea of Biblical Worship,* and Arthurs, *Devote Yourself.*

Bibliography

Allen, Ronald J. *Preaching and Practical Ministry.* St. Louis: Chalice, 2001.

Alston, Wallace M., Jr. "What a Minister is to Do." In *From Midterms to Ministry: Practical Theologians on Pastoral Beginnings,* edited by Allan Hugh Cole, Jr., 250–62. Grand Rapids: Eerdmans, 2008.

The American Heritage Dictionary. Rev. ed. Boston: Houghton Mifflin, 1985.

Arthurs, Jeffrey D. *Devote Yourself to the Public Reading of Scripture.* Grand Rapids: Kregel, 2012.

Association of Religious Data Archives. http://www.thearda.com/ConQS/qs_295.asp.

Association of Theological Schools. https://ats.edu/.

Ball, Roger. "Initiating Dialogue." In *Dear Pastor, Ministry Advice from Seasoned Pastors,* edited by John R. Cionca, 125–28. Loveland, CO: Group, 2007.

Batten, Patricia. *Parenting by Faith: What Jesus Said to Parents.* Peabody, MA: Rose, 2019.

Best-Boss, Angie. *Surviving Your First Year as Pastor: What Seminary Couldn't Teach You.* Valley Forge, PA: Judson, 1999.

Biebel, David B., and Harold G. Koenig. *Simple Health: Easy and Inexpensive Things You Can Do to Improve Your Health.* Lake Mary, FL: Siloam, 2005.

Blanchard, Ken, and Phil Hodges. *Lead Like Jesus: Lessons from the Greatest Leadership Role Model of All Times.* Waco, TX: W, 2005.

Bloem, Steve. *The Pastoral Handbook of Mental Illness: A Guide for Training and Reference.* Grand Rapids: Kregel, 2018.

Boehi, David, et al. *Preparing for Marriage: The Complete Guide to Help You Discover God's Plan for a Lifetime of Love.* Ventura, CA: Gospel Light, 1997.

Bonem, Mike, and Roger Patterson. *Leading from the Second Chair: Serving Your Church, Fulfilling Your Role, and Realizing Your Dreams.* San Francisco: Jossey-Bass, 2005.

Brown, Sally A. *Sunday's Sermon for Monday's World: Preaching to Shape Daring Witness.* Grand Rapids: Eerdmans, 2020.

Buchanan, John M. Foreword to *Ministry Loves Company: A Survival Guide for Pastors,* by John Galloway, Jr., ix–xiv. Louisville: Westminster John Knox, 2003.

Burg, Bob, and John David Mann. *The Go-Giver Leader: A Little Story About What Matters Most in Business.* New York: Portfolio, 2016.

Butterfield, Rosaria. *The Gospel Comes with a House Key: Practicing Radically Ordinary Hospitality in Our Post-Christian World*. Wheaton, IL: Crossway, 2018.

Byun, Eddie. *Praying for Your Pastor: How Your Prayer Support is Their Life Support*. Downers Grove, IL: InterVarsity, 2016.

Chapman, Gary. *The Five Love Languages: How to Express Heartfelt Commitment to Your Mate*. Chicago: Northfield, 2004.

Cloud, Henry, and John Townsend. *Boundaries: When to Say Yes, How to Say No to Take Control of Your Life*. Grand Rapids: Zondervan, 1992.

Cole, Allan Hugh, Jr., ed. *From Midterms to Ministry: Practical Theologians on Pastoral Beginnings*. Grand Rapids: Eerdmans, 2008.

Collins, Travis. *What Does it Mean to Be Welcoming?: Navigating LGBT Questions in Your Church*. Downers Grove, IL: InterVarsity, 2018.

Covenant Eyes. https://www.covenanteyes.com/services/.

Cullen, Lisa Takeuchi. "Pastors' Wives Come Together." *Time*, April 9, 2007, 46–48.

Currie, David A. *The Big Idea of Biblical Worship: The Development and Leadership of Expository Services*. Peabody, MA: Hendrickson, 2017.

Daley, Jerome. *Gravitas: The Monastic Rhythms of Healthy Leadership*. Colorado Springs, CO: NavPress, 2020.

Daman, Glenn C. *Leading the Small Church: How to Develop a Transformational Ministry*. Grand Rapids: Kregel, 2006.

———. *Shepherding the Small Church: A Leadership Guide for the Majority of Today's Churches*. 2d ed. Grand Rapids: Kregel, 2008.

Davison, Lisa Wilson. *Preaching the Women of the Bible*. St. Louis: Chalice, 2006.

DeGroat, Chuck. *When Narcissism Comes to Church: Healing Your Community From Emotional and Spiritual Abuse*. Downers Grove, IL: InterVarsity, 2020.

Demarest, Bruce. *Satisfy Your Soul: Restoring the Heart of Christian Spirituality*. Colorado Springs, CO: NavPress, 1999.

DeMuth, Mary E. *We Too: How the Church Can Respond Redemptively to the Sexual Abuse Crisis*. Eugene, OR: Harvest House, 2019.

Doehring, Carrie. "Fragile Connections: Constructing an Identity in the First Year of Ministry." In *From Midterms to Ministry: Practical Theologians on Pastoral Beginnings*, edited by Allan Hugh Cole, Jr., 99–103. Grand Rapids: Eerdmans, 2008.

Dunlop, Jamie. *Budgeting for a Healthy Church: Aligning Finances with Biblical Priorities for Ministry*. Grand Rapids: Zondervan, 2019.

Edwards, Judson. *The Leadership Labyrinth: Negotiating the Paradoxes of Ministry*. Macon, GA: Smyth & Helwys, 2005.

Elliff, Jim. "The Cure of Souls: The Pastor Serving the Flock." In *Reforming Pastoral Ministry: Challenges for Ministry in Postmodern Times*, edited by John H. Armstrong, 147–66. Wheaton, IL: Crossway, 2001.

Ells, Alfred. *The Resilient Leader: How Adversity Can Change You and Your Ministry for the Better*. Colorado Springs, CO: Cook, 2020.

Encyclopedia Britannica. "Apprenticeship." https://www.britannica.com/topic/apprenticeship.

Everhart, Ruth. *The #MeToo Reckoning: Facing the Church's Complicity in Sexual Abuse and Misconduct*. Downers Grove, IL: InterVarsity, 2020.

Ford, Leighton. *Transforming Leadership: Jesus' Way of Creating Vision, Shaping Values, and Empowering Change*. Downers Grove, IL: InterVarsity, 1991.

Forman, Rowland, et al. *The Leadership Baton: An Intentional Strategy for Developing Leaders in Your Church.* Grand Rapids: Zondervan, 2004.

Foster, Charles R., et al. *Educating Clergy: Teaching Practices and Pastoral Imagination.* San Francisco: Jossey-Bass, 2006.

Foster, Richard. *Prayer: Finding the Heart's True Home.* San Francisco: Harper Collins, 1992.

Fries, Micah, and Jeremy Maxfield. *Leveling the Church: Multiplying Your Ministry by Giving It Away.* Chicago: Moody, 2020.

Gallaty, Robby, and Chris Swain. *Replicate: How to Create a Culture of Disciple-Making Right Where You Are.* Chicago: Moody, 2020.

Galloway, John, Jr. *Ministry Loves Company: A Survival Guide for Pastors.* Louisville: Westminster John Knox, 2003.

Gibbons, Dave. *The Monkey and the Fish: Liquid Leadership for a Third-Culture Church.* Grand Rapids: Zondervan, 2009.

Gibson, Scott M. "The Character of Preaching." Class notes: Preaching, Gordon-Conwell Theological Seminary.

———. "The Landscape of the Character of Preaching." In *Midwestern Journal of Theology* 14 (2005) 16–37.

———. "The Preacher's Character." *Preaching: The Professional Journal for Ministry Leaders* 35 (2020) 12–16.

———. *Preaching with a Plan: Sermon Strategies for Growing Mature Believers.* Grand Rapids: Baker, 2012.

———. *Should We Use Someone Else's Sermon? Preaching in a Cut-and-Paste World.* Grand Rapids: Zondervan, 2008.

Green, Michael P. *Illustrations for Biblical Preaching.* 3rd ed. Grand Rapids: Baker, 1989.

Gupta, Nijay K. *Prepare, Succeed, Advance: A Guidebook for Getting a PhD in Biblical Studies and Beyond.* 2d ed. Eugene, OR: Cascade, 2019.

Hansen, David. *The Art of Pastoring: Ministry Without All the Answers.* Downers Grove, IL: InterVarsity, 1994.

Hedahl, Susan K. *Listening Ministry: Rethinking Pastoral Leadership.* Minneapolis: Fortress, 2001.

Helopoulos, Jason. *The New Pastor's Handbook: Help and Encouragement for the First Years of Ministry.* Grand Rapids: Baker, 2015.

Henderson, Daniel. *Glorious Finish: Keeping Your Eye on the Prize of Eternity in a Time of Pastoral Failings.* Chicago: Moody, 2020.

Herrington, Jim, et al. *Leading Congregational Change: A Practical Guide for the Transformational Journey.* San Francisco: Jossey-Bass, 2000.

Hillman, George M., Jr., and John Reece. *Smart Church Finances: A Pastor's Guide to Budgets: Spreadsheets, and Other Things You Didn't Learn in Seminary.* Bellingham, WA: Lexham, 2020.

Hoge, Dean R., and Jacqueline E. Wenger. *Pastors in Transition: Why Clergy Leave Local Church Ministry.* Grand Rapids: Eerdmans, 2005.

Horn, David. *Soulmates: Friendship, Fellowship, and the Making of Christian Community.* Peabody, MA: Hendrickson, 2017.

Horner, David. *A Practical Guide for Life and Ministry: Overcoming 7 Challenges Pastors Face.* Grand Rapids: Baker, 2008.

Hughes, R. Kent. *The Pastor's Book: A Comprehensive and Practical Guide to Pastoral Ministry.* Wheaton, IL: Crossway, 2015.

Hughes, R. Kent, and Barbara Hughes. *Liberating Ministry from the Success Syndrome*. Rev. ed. Wheaton, IL: Crossway, 2008.

Huguley, Ryan. *8 Hours or Less: Writing Faithful Sermons Faster*. Chicago: Moody, 2017.

Hulme, William E., et al. *Pastors in Ministry: Guidelines for Seven Critical Issues*. Minneapolis: Augsburg, 1985.

Hummel, Charles E. *Tyranny of the Urgent*. Downers Grove, IL: InterVarsity, 1994.

Im, Daniel. *No Silver Bullets: Five Small Shifts That Will Transform Your Ministry*. Nashville: B&H, 2017.

———. *You Are What You Do: And Six Other Lies About Work, Life, and Love*. Nashville: B&H, 2020.

Iorg, Jeff. *Is God Calling Me?: Answering the Question Every Leader Asks*. Nashville: B&H, 2008.

Jackson, Anne. *Mad Church Disease: Overcoming the Burnout Epidemic*. Grand Rapids: Zondervan, 2009.

Jethani, Skye. *Immeasurable: Reflections on the Soul of Ministry in the Age of Church, Inc*. Chicago: Moody, 2017.

Jinkins, Michael. *Letters to New Pastors*. Grand Rapids: Eerdmans, 2006.

Jones, L. Gregory, and Kevin R. Armstrong. *Resurrecting Excellence: Shaping Faithful Christian Ministry*. Grand Rapids: Eerdmans, 2006.

Jones, L. Gregory, and Susan Pendleton Jones. "Leadership, Pastoral Identity, and Friendship: Navigating the Transition from Seminary to the Parish." In *From Midterms to Ministry: Practical Theologians on Pastoral Beginnings*, edited by Allan Hugh Cole, Jr., 13–26. Grand Rapids: Eerdmans, 2008.

Kaelin, Louise Morganti. "Legalize Your Emotions." http://www.livinglifefully.com/flo/flolegalizeyouremotions.htm.

Kim, Matthew D. *Becoming a Friendlier Church*. Bellingham, WA: Lexham, forthcoming.

———. *A Little Book for New Preachers: Why and How to Study Homiletics*. Downers Grove, IL: IVP Academic, 2020.

———. *Preaching to People in Pain: How Suffering Can Shape Your Sermons and Connect with Your Congregation*. Grand Rapids: Baker Academic, 2021.

———. *Preaching with Cultural Intelligence: Understanding the People Who Hear Our Sermons*. Grand Rapids: Baker Academic, 2017.

Kinnaman, David. "The Porn Phenomenon." Barna, February 5, 2016. https://www.barna.com/the-porn-phenomenon/.

Kinnaman, Gary D., and Alfred H. Ells. *Leaders That Last: How Covenant Friendships Can Help Pastors Thrive*. Grand Rapids: Baker, 2003.

Kreider, Larry. *Authentic Spiritual Mentoring: Nurturing Believers Toward Spiritual Maturity*. Ventura, CA: Regal, 2008.

Langford, Daniel L. *The Pastor's Family: The Challenges of Family Life and Pastoral Responsibilities*. New York: Haworth Pastoral, 1998.

Lake, Mac. *The Multiplication Effect: Building a Leadership Pipeline That Solves Your Leadership Shortage*. Nashville: Thomas Nelson, 2020.

Linhart, Terry. *The Self-Aware Leader: Discovering Your Blind Spots to Reach Your Ministry Potential*. Downers Grove, IL: InterVarsity, 2017.

Long, Thomas G. "The Essential Untidiness of Ministry." In *From Midterms to Ministry: Practical Theologians on Pastoral Beginnings*, edited by Allan Hugh Cole, Jr., 1–12. Grand Rapids: Eerdmans, 2008.

Lummis, Adair T. "What Do Lay People Want in Pastors? Answers from Lay Search Committee Chairs and Regional Judicatory Leaders." In *Pulpit and Pew Research Reports*, 6–24. Durham, NC: Duke Divinity School, 2003. https://faithandleadership. com/programs/spe/resources/ppr/pastorsearch.pdf.

Lutzer, Erwin. *Pastor to Pastor: Tackling the Problems of Ministry*. Rev. ed. Grand Rapids: Kregel, 1998.

Malphurs, Aubrey, and Will Mancini. *Building Leaders: Blueprints for Developing Leadership at Every Level of Your Church*. 3rd ed. Grand Rapids: Baker, 2006.

Maslach, Christina, and Susan E. Jackson. "The Measurement of Experienced Burnout." *Journal of Occupational Behaviour* 2 (1981) 99–113.

Massey, James Earl. *The Burdensome Joy of Preaching*. Nashville: Abingdon, 1998.

Maxwell, John C. *The 21 Indispensable Qualities of a Leader: Becoming the Person Others Will Want to Follow*. Nashville: Thomas Nelson, 1999.

McGee, Robert S. *The Search for Significance: Seeing Your True Worth through God's Eyes*. Nashville: W, 2003.

McIntosh, Gary L. *Beyond the First Visit: The Complete Guide to Connecting Guests to Your Church*. Grand Rapids: Baker, 2006.

McKnight, Scot. *Pastor Paul: Nurturing a Culture of Christoformity in the Church*. Grand Rapids: Brazos, 2019.

Menikoff, Aaron. *Character Matters: Shepherding in the Fruit of the Spirit*. Chicago: Moody, 2020.

Merriam Webster Dictionary. "Cultivate." https://www.merriam-webster.com/dictionary/ cultivate.

Miller, Jeffrey E. *Hazards of Being a Man: Overcoming 12 Challenges All Men Face*. Grand Rapids: Baker, 2007.

Millican, Nate, and Jonathan Woodyard, eds. *Before We Forget: Reflections from New and Seasoned Pastors on Enduring Ministry*. Nashville: B&H, 2020.

Milton, Michael. "Portrait of a Minister." In *Preaching: The Professional Journal for Preachers* 24 (2009) 40. https://www.preaching.com/sermons/portrait-of-a-minister -1-timothy-46-16/.

Minirth, Frank, et al. *What They Didn't Teach You in Seminary*. Nashville: Thomas Nelson, 1993.

Mounce, William D., ed. *Mounce's Complete Expository Dictionary of Old and New Testament Words*. Grand Rapids: Zondervan, 2006.

Nieuwhof, Carey. "5 Reasons Pastors Fail Morally (And What to Watch for in Your Own Life)." https://careynieuwhof.com/5-reasons-pastors-fail-morally-and-what-to-watch -for-in-your-own-life/.

Oswald, Roy M. *Clergy Self-Care: Finding a Balance for Effective Ministry*. New York: Alban Institute, 1991.

Padilla, Kristen. *Now That I'm Called: A Guide for Women Discerning a Call to Ministry*. Grand Rapids: Zondervan, 2018.

Perkins, Bill. *When Good Men Are Tempted*. Rev. ed. Grand Rapids: Zondervan, 2007.

Peterson, Eugene H. *Five Smooth Stones for Pastoral Work*. Grand Rapids: Eerdmans, 1980.

———. *Working the Angles: The Shape of Pastoral Integrity*. Grand Rapids: Eerdmans, 1987.

Piper, Barnabas. *The Pastor's Kid: Finding Your Own Faith and Identity*. Colorado Springs, CO: Cook, 2014.

Platt, David. *Follow Him: A 35-Day Call to Live for Christ No Matter the Cost*. Carol Stream, IL: Tyndale Momentum, 2020.

Prime, Derek, and Alistair Begg. *On Being a Pastor: Understanding Our Calling and Work*. Chicago: Moody, 2004.

Proeschold-Bell, Rae Jean, and Jason Byassee. *Faithful and Fractured: Responding to the Clergy Health Crisis*. Grand Rapids: Baker Academic, 2018.

Purves, Andrew. *The Crucifixion of Ministry: Surrendering our Ambitions to the Service of Christ*. Downers Grove, IL: InterVarsity, 2007.

Putnam, Robert D. *Bowling Alone: The Collapse and Revival of American Community*. New York: Simon & Schuster, 2000.

Rah, Soong-Chan. *The Next Evangelicalism: Freeing the Church from Western Cultural Captivity*. Downers Grove, IL: InterVarsity, 2009.

Rainer, Thom S. *Becoming a Welcoming Church*. Nashville: B&H, 2018.

———. "How Much Time Do Pastors Spend on Preparing a Sermon?" June 22, 2013. https://thomrainer.com/2013/06/how-much-time-do-pastors-spend-preparing-sermon/.

Rediger, G. Lloyd. *Clergy Killers: Guidance for Pastors and Congregations Under Attack*. Louisville: Westminster John Knox, 1997.

Reed, Rick. *The Heart of the Preacher: Preparing Your Soul to Proclaim the Word*. Bellingham, WA: Lexham, 2019.

Robert, Dana. *Faithful Friendships: Embracing Diversity in Christian Community*. Grand Rapids: Eerdmans, 2019.

Robert, Henry M., III, et al. *Robert's Rules of Order: Newly Revised*. 12th ed. New York: PublicAffairs, 2020.

Robinson, Haddon. "Preaching Priorities." In *Dear Pastor: Ministry Advice from Seasoned Pastors*, edited by John R. Cionca, 154–56. Loveland, CO: Group, 2007.

Sanchez, Juan. *The Leadership Formula: Develop the Next Generation of Leaders in the Church*. Nashville: B&H, 2020.

Sbanotto, Elisabeth A. Nesbit, and Craig Blomberg. *Effective Generational Ministry: Biblical and Practical Insights for Transforming Church Communities*. Grand Rapids: Baker Academic, 2016.

Scazzero, Pete. "Skimming." http://www.christianitytoday.com/le/thepastor/soulspirit/skimming.html?start=3.

Senkbeil, Harold L. *The Care of Souls: Cultivating a Pastor's Heart*. Bellingham, WA: Lexham, 2019.

Seymour, Jody. *A Time for Healing: Overcoming the Perils of Ministry*. Valley Forge, PA: Judson, 1995.

Shelley, Marshall. *The Healthy Hectic Home: Raising a Family in the Midst of Ministry*. Carol Stream, IL: Christianity Today, 1988.

Shellnutt, Kate. "Beyond Cedarville: Why Do Pastors Keep Getting Rehired After Abuse?" *Christianity Today*, April 28, 2020. https://www.christianitytoday.com/news/2020/april/cedarville-white-anthony-moore-christian-leaders-abuse.html.

Shriver, Dean. *Nobody's Perfect, But You Have to Be: The Power of Personal Integrity in Effective Preaching*. Grand Rapids: Baker, 2005.

Sisk, Ronald D. *The Competent Pastor: Skills and Self-Knowledge for Serving Well*. Herndon, VA: Alban Institute, 2005.

Small, Ebony S. *The Leader in You: Discovering Your Unexpected Path to Influence*. Downers Grove, IL: InterVarsity, 2020.

Smith, Gordon T. *Wisdom from Babylon: Leadership for the Church in a Secular Age.* Downers Grove, IL: IVP Academic, 2020.

Smith, Mandy. *The Vulnerable Pastor: How Human Limitations Empower Our Ministry.* Downers Grove, IL: InterVarsity, 2015.

Smith, William P. *How to Love Difficult People: Receiving and Sharing God's Mercy.* Greensboro, NC: New Growth, 2008.

Stetzer, Ed, and Mike Dodson. "Producing a Comeback Church." In *Preaching: The Professional Journal for Preachers* 23 (2008) 38.

Stevens, R. Paul. *Liberating the Laity: Equipping All the Saints for Ministry.* Vancouver: Regent College, 1993.

Stone, Charles. *People-Pleasing Pastors: Avoiding the Pitfalls of Approval-Motivated Leadership.* Downers Grove, IL: InterVarsity, 2014.

Swetland, Kenneth L. "God Is God and We Are Not." Chapel Sermon. Gordon-Conwell Theological Seminary, South Hamilton, MA, April 16, 2008.

———. *The Hidden World of the Pastor: Case Studies on Personal Issues of Real Pastors.* Eugene, OR: Wipf & Stock, 2007.

Talley, Doug. "Listen to Your Spouse." In *Dear Pastor: Ministry Advice from Seasoned Pastors,* edited by John R. Cionca, 73–76. Loveland, CO: Group, 2007.

Tan, Siang-Yang. *Shepherding God's People: A Guide to Faithful and Fruitful Pastoral Ministry.* Grand Rapids: Baker Academic, 2019.

Thomas, Curtis C. *Practical Wisdom for Pastors: Words of Encouragement and Counsel for a Lifetime of Ministry.* Wheaton, IL: Crossway, 2001.

Thomas, John C., ed. *Counseling Techniques: A Comprehensive Resource for Christian Counselors.* Grand Rapids: Zondervan, 2018.

Tidball, Derek. *Skillful Shepherds: An Introduction to Pastoral Theology.* Grand Rapids: Zondervan, 1986.

Tisdale, Leonora Tubbs. *Preaching as Local Theology and Folk Art.* Minneapolis: Fortress, 1997.

Tripp, Paul David. *Lead: 12 Gospel Principles for Leadership in the Church.* Wheaton, IL: Crossway, 2020.

Van Dyk, Leanne. "Learning the Life of the Pastor." In *Preaching: The Professional Journal for Preachers* 24 (2009) 32.

Vanderbloemen, William, and Warren Bird. *Next: Pastoral Succession That Works.* Expanded and updated ed. Grand Rapids: Baker, 2020.

Vawter, John. "Handling Criticism." In *Dear Pastor, Ministry Advice from Seasoned Pastors,* edited by John R. Cionca, 143–46. Loveland, CO: Group, 2007.

Wagner, E. Glenn. *Escape from Church, Inc.: The Return of the Pastor-Shepherd.* Grand Rapids: Zondervan, 1999.

Ward, Angie. "From First Chair to Second Fiddle: Your Calling to Ministry May Lead from Senior Pastor to Associate." In *Leadership* 28 (Winter 2007) 81–83. http://www .christianitytoday.com/le/2007/001/4.81.html.

———. *I Am a Leader: When Women Discover the Joy of Their Calling.* Colorado Springs, CO: NavPress, 2020.

Warren, Tish Harrison. "It's Not Billy Graham Rule or Bust." *Christianity Today,* April 27, 2018. https://www.christianitytoday.com/ct/2018/april-web-only/its-not-billy-graham-rule-or-bust.html

Whitehurst, Teresa. *How Would Jesus Raise a Child?* Grand Rapids: Baker, 2003.

Willhite, Keith. *Preaching with Relevance: Without Dumbing Down.* Grand Rapids: Kregel, 2001.

Willimon, William H. *Pastor: The Theology and Practice of Ordained Ministry.* Nashville: Abingdon, 2002.

Wilson, Michael Todd, and Brad Hoffman. *Preventing Ministry Failure: A ShepherdCare Guide for Pastors, Ministers, and Other Caregivers.* Downers Grove, IL: InterVarsity, 2007.

Wingard, Charles Malcolm. *Help for the New Pastor: Practical Advice for Your First Year of Ministry.* Phillipsburg, NJ: P&R, 2018.

Witmer, Stephen. *A Big Gospel in Small Places: Why Ministry in Forgotten Communities Matters.* Downers Grove, IL: InterVarsity, 2019.

Yancey, George. *One Body One Spirit: Principles of Successful Multiracial Churches.* Downers Grove, IL: InterVarsity, 2003.

www.ingramcontent.com/pod-product-compliance
Lightning Source LLC
Chambersburg PA
CBHW021151160426
42812CB00078B/614